Praise for
Soul Obsession

"*Soul Obsession* is a call to arms for the body of Christ. Nicky Cruz's captivating accounts of his God-inspired, passionate pursuit for souls challenges us to trust God with bold, childlike faith and to love others with sincere mercy and deep compassion. This book fans the embers of complacency! You will be reignited, challenged, and inspired by this outstanding book."

—JOHN BEVERE, author, speaker, and president
of Messenger International

"A page turner! I was challenged as Nicky Cruz took me through his pursuit of God until it became his life's driving passion. You'll also catch an inside look into his background in Puerto Rico and his evangelistic crusades from Norway to Hawaii. If you have read the *Cross and the Switchblade* and *Run, Baby, Run,* you will not want to miss *Soul Obsession!*"

—ROBERT STRAND, speaker and author of *Angel*
at My Door and other books

"In *Soul Obsession,* Nicky Cruz tells stories from his life and ministry that will revolutionize your view of people. Nicky's unique experiences and exposure to people from all walks of life put him in an authoritative position to comment on God's heart for the lost. If you want to see your ministry grow in power, make sure you're pursuing what God is pursuing: his people."

—TED HAGGARD, senior pastor of New Life Church

SOUL
OBSESSION

SOUL
OBSESSION

When God's Primary Pursuit Becomes Your Life's Driving Passion

NICKY CRUZ

with Frank Martin

WATERBROOK
PRESS

SOUL OBSESSION
PUBLISHED BY WATERBROOK PRESS
2375 Telstar Drive, Suite 160
Colorado Springs, Colorado 80920
A division of Random House, Inc.

Scripture quotations are taken from the *Holy Bible, New International Version*®. NIV®. Copyright © 1973, 1978, 1984 by International Bible Society. Used by permission of Zondervan Publishing House. All rights reserved.

Details in some anecdotes and stories have been changed to protect the identities of the persons involved.

ISBN 1-57856-893-5

WATERBROOK and its deer design logo are registered trademarks of WaterBrook Press, a division of Random House, Inc.

Library of Congress Cataloging-in-Publication Data
Cruz, Nicky.
    Soul obsession : when God's primary pursuit becomes your life's driving passion / Nicky Cruz with Frank Martin.— 1st ed.
      p. cm.
    ISBN 1-57856-893-5
  1. Christian life. 2. God—Worship and love. I. Martin, Frank, 1958– II. Title.
    BV4501.3.C78 2005
    248.4—dc22

                                 2004029442

Printed in the United States of America
2005—First Edition

10 9 8 7 6 5 4 3 2 1

This book is dedicated to several people who have touched my soul.

—

BOBBY AND ROSE CRUZ

Bobby is the founding pastor of House of Prayer Church in Miami, Florida. He came from the secular world of entertainment and is known as the father of salsa music. Bobby along with Richie Ray invented salsa music. There was a time when they were as popular as The Beatles, and their popularity remains very strong to this day. They are loved not only in Puerto Rico, but all the Latin American countries as well as Europe and Japan. I've been to their concerts with stadiums filled to capacity and witnessed as they stopped the concert to share about Jesus and His love. During these times they don't pull any punches and they always offer the opportunity to accept Christ. Bobby is so sensitive to the leading of the Holy Spirit, and I consider it an honor to call him my friend and spiritual son.

SONNY AND JULIE ARGUINZONI

As the founder of Victory Outreach International, Sonny has brought dignity to the unwanted for over thirty-five years. Victory Outreach has founded more than five hundred churches worldwide and done more to save kids from drugs and alcohol than any ministry I'm aware of. Jesus took Sonny, a former addict, and made him a powerful man of God. Sonny will always hold a special place in my heart. To me, he is like Mother Teresa—he opens the fields of hope to the poor and downcast. Sonny is my spiritual son, and I love him like a brother.

MARILU AND CARLOS DONES REYES

Together they cofounded the Bethel Baptist Church in Puerto Rico more than thirty years ago—a church they faithfully pastor to this day. Like me, they believe in doing whatever it takes to spread the gospel and lead people to Jesus. They are completely sold out to God and to their community. Marilu and Carlos are people of prayer, principle, and character—never compromising, never giving up. I am so proud to have them as my friends!

VICTOR AND CARMEN TORRES

Victor is my spiritual son; he was saved while at Teen Challenge in New York City when I was the director. Victor and his wife, Carmen, are the founding pastors of New Life Outreach International, a growing church in Richmond, Virginia. I am proud of them; they've come a long way. Through the good, the bad, and the in-between, they have persevered and remained consistent in their walk with the Lord. They are true examples that integrity in ministry pays off, which is evidenced in their service to God.

REGGIE WHITE

Reggie went home to be with the Lord in December, 2004. What an incredible man of God he was! Reggie had such a gift for winning people to Jesus. He was always witnessing to everyone and was especially committed to reaching other African Americans. Reggie's life was a testimony to the world and most effectively to those who followed sports. I knew Reggie as a very generous man, as a man who walked with Christ and never compromised. To Sara and their children, Jeremy and Jecolia, I loved Reggie, he was my friend and I will miss him.

FRANK BAEZ

Frank was my spiritual son who recently went home to be with the Lord. The amazing thing about Frank was the humbleness of his life. Of the thirteen that I sent to school, Frank went a different direction. His only support came from me and Jesus. Frank was true to his salvation, his calling, and to his beautiful wife, Lolita. Frank will be missed not only by me, but by many others, including his family and home congregation in Brighton, Colorado.

CONTENTS

SOUL
OBSESSION

REDEEMED BY LOVE

I was twenty-two years old when I received word that my mother was dying, and I wasn't prepared for the mixed feelings this news would elicit within me.

I was living in New York at the time, still a relatively new baby in the faith, and serving as the head of Teen Challenge Ministries. My mother was in Las Piedras, Puerto Rico, on her deathbed in the tiny stucco home where I had grown up. Most of my seventeen brothers and one sister were already at her side by the time the news reached me.

I wished I could have said that I loved my mother at the time, but I couldn't. If anything, my feelings toward her ranged from hate to indifference. I'd spent much of my childhood hiding from her and the balance of it getting away from her. To me she symbolized everything that I despised about my past.

I wanted so much to forget the many times she had beaten me and cursed at me. I felt detested by her, even as a young boy. I remember standing before her once as she called me a "child of the devil" in front of her friends. She made me feel like nothing, a waste of space on the earth, a mistake, an ugly child who should never have been born.

For so many years I longed to get close to my mother, to hold her, to feel her kiss on my cheek. But Satan had such a grip on her heart that she didn't know how to love, and I didn't know how to love her back. Evil had taken hold in her spirit, and it wouldn't let her go. Wouldn't allow her to be the mother that I so desperately wanted and needed.

And now she was dying. *Was I supposed to be sad? to cry? to pretend that I loved her and run to her side like any good son would do?* I honestly didn't know. But deep in my heart I did know what Jesus would do. He would go see his dying mother. So I booked a flight to Puerto Rico.

I had forgotten how beautiful Puerto Rico could be. Growing up in such darkness and horror, I had never learned to appreciate the picturesque surroundings of our little island in the Atlantic. Las Piedras is perfectly nestled in a valley of lush green, framed by untold beauty. You feel as if you could reach out with one arm and embrace the magnificent El Yunque Mountains, and with the other allow your fingers to swim along the aqua blue waters of the ocean. We used to call this place "The Rainfall." It's one of the most stunning places on earth.

Seeing my parents' house for the first time in seven years was a bit of a shock for me. The place looked so small and insignificant. Like any other house on the block. But in my heart I knew that wasn't true. This house was evil to the core, filled with horrible memories and unspeakable pain. Every crevice harbored demons of abuse and neglect—demons that still lingered, roaming the halls at night, haunting like a bad nightmare. I could feel them in my bones.

Behind the home, about a hundred yards into the woods, still stood the large round building—the place that so frightened me as a child and now sent chills to the center of my being. As a boy I knew it only as the "Spirit House," the place where my mother and father went regularly to summon the healing spirits. The town was convinced that they knew what went on here, and rumors ran thick throughout Puerto Rico, but few had seen it up close and personal. They suspected evil and talked of the hideous things going on inside the infamous Spirit House; I had seen it firsthand.

As I stood staring at the large round building framed by trees, the memories began to rise to the surface. Memories of strange and unexplainable things that happened here on a regular basis—things that I still resist speaking of, all these years later.

My father was a spiritist—some say the most powerful in all of Puerto Rico—and my mother was a medium. So many times I watched helplessly from outside the window as their bizarre séances raged out of control. People inside would wail and moan and scream, summoning the spirits of the dead to awaken in their presence. Sometimes these spirits would take over my mother's body, turning her face white and her eyes violently yellow. Once I saw an evil spirit come upon her with such force that it catapulted her through the air. Though she was a small woman, it took four or five men to contain her.

Another time I saw my father become possessed by a spirit he couldn't control. He grabbed my youngest brother, put a rope around his neck, and tried to hang him from the limb of a tree. It took the combined strength of the whole family to hold him down as my brother slipped free. Later my father had no memory of the ordeal. In his right mind he would never have done such a thing to his children.

Even at a young age I understood the dangers of dabbling in the occult. Yet I found myself living in a home that did far more than dabble. We were known throughout the island as the home of *El Taumaturgo* (the Wonder

Worker, the Great One). The place you go to find the warlock and the witch of Las Piedras.

BOUND BY PAIN

I couldn't remember how many times I had sworn never to come back—never again to darken the evil doors of my parents' home. Yet here I was. And my mother was dying. As I slipped through the small corridors of our house, I could feel the satanic forces surrounding the house, the forces that had kept my family bound in darkness for so many years.

My mother didn't recognize me the first time I walked into her bedroom. I can still see her lying there, babbling incoherently, with sweat pouring down the sides of her face. I tried to talk to her, but she just stared at me, her eyes cold and empty. Lifeless eyes. Loveless eyes.

"Mama, it's me, Nicky," I said to her several times. She didn't respond, just stared right through me as if I wasn't there.

As if she were possessed by some ancient, evil spirit.

The sight of my mother's dark and wicked gaze was more than I could handle, so I turned and fled. I told my father I would be back, but I wasn't sure I meant it. *Why am I even here?* I thought. *She doesn't love me; she doesn't even know me. Her days of evil have caught up with her, and now she's facing God's judgment. Who am I to interfere?*

I took off walking down the street, down the long road leading away from my parents' house, away from the evil that hovered and haunted all around. The whole time I was there I could feel Satan taunting me, touching me, grabbing at my clothes. My parents' home was a rathole of evil, and I could feel it with every fiber of my being. I had to get away, to escape the forces of oppression attacking me.

4

I considered catching an early flight back to New York, back to Gloria and my new life in God's service. People there needed me—people at Teen Challenge, the ministry that God had called me to. There they understood me. They knew that I was no longer a slave to my past, no longer bound to the hate and abuse of my childhood. No longer the "child of the devil" that my mother had tried to make me.

She deserves this fate. She will die as she lived—surrounded by sin and possessed by evil. I can't help her now. No one can. She worshiped Satan on earth, now she will spend an eternity licking his boots in hell!

As I walked along the lush green valley, listening to the birds singing and the animals scurrying through the woods, the farther I got from the house the more peaceful things became. The scent of Satan grew dimmer with each step. I had every intention of leaving, of going back to New York and forgetting my mother forever, of going on with my life and putting my past behind me. Yet somewhere, deep in my spirit, I knew I couldn't. God wouldn't let me go. I knew I had to go back.

Suddenly I heard the sound of singing in the distance. Beautiful voices, echoing through the wind, like songs of praise. I remembered a church not far from my parents' home. It was Monday evening, and I didn't expect anyone to be in church, yet the sounds grew stronger as I drew nearer. *I need to be around other believers,* I thought. *People like me. Maybe they can pray with me—pray for me. Give me some spiritual support before I have to face those evil eyes again!*

A CRY FOR HELP

I walked to the church and sat in the back. They were having testimonies, so I sat and listened until there was an appropriate opportunity for me to rise and make a statement about my family. The pastor didn't know me, so as I stood, I introduced myself. I said, "My name is Nicky Cruz, son of Don Galo and Aleja Velazques Cruz. I want to ask you to come to my house to pray for my mother."

"Welcome, Nicky," he said, and we embraced.

A group gathered around us as I told him of my dying mother. I explained my need for prayers and support, and as I was speaking, I repeated, "Pastor, would you be willing to come with me and pray for my mother?"

Before he had a chance to answer, I turned to those standing nearby and asked, "Would any of you come and pray for my mother?"

No one said a word. The silence was deafening, and several stepped back. Suddenly one woman moved forward—a woman with fire in her eyes and hate in her voice. "We cannot go to that house," she said. "That house is evil. That man and woman are demon-possessed. All their children are evil. Even their dog is possessed by the devil. We will not go near that place."

My heart sank. I glanced around the room, and no one would look at me. All eyes fell to the floor, sheepishly. It wasn't apathy I sensed but fear. Everyone knew what went on at the Spirit House.

I caught the pastor's eyes and locked onto them. Then in one last effort, I said to him, "Pastor, I'm going to ask you again. Are you willing to come to my house and pray for my mother?"

The pastor's gaze floated around the room as he considered his response. One by one he looked at those standing nearby. Everyone waited for his response. He turned to me and said, "Nicky, you know I will be there."

Again he surveyed his small flock, including the woman who had spoken so harshly, then added, "We'll all be there."

An Unexpected Miracle

We had scheduled to meet at my mother's house around seven the next evening, and by seven thirty no one had shown up. I waited on the front porch, watching the long road winding to my parents' home, yet no one came. *They're not coming,* I thought. *The pastor couldn't convince anyone to venture near the evil Spirit House.*

At eight o'clock I rose to my feet, discouraged, deflated. Feeling abandoned and alone. *I should have known they would be too frightened to come.*

I walked toward my parents' front door but, before opening it, turned to look one last time down the road. In the distance I caught sight of some people walking toward the house. Not just a few, but dozens of people. The line kept growing and growing. Within minutes people were flocking toward the house, playing guitars and tambourines. The sweet fragrance of their music filled the air around us.

Soon our yard was packed with fellow villagers, not thirty or fifty, as I had hoped, but several hundred! Never had our small home seen so many visitors. They came from all directions, introducing themselves to me as they arrived. There were Methodists, Pentecostals, Lutherans, Presbyterians, Catholics, all faiths and denominations, from all over our little town of Las Piedras, coming to pray for my mother. And they didn't come for a quick visit; they came to rumble with the devil!

I could hardly contain the tears as people kept arriving, flooding into my mother's home by the dozens. When the house could hold no more, they surrounded the yard and locked hands. A circle of believers swallowed our tiny home. All around, believers were laying hands on the house, anointing it with oils of blessing, praying for protection and deliverance from evil. My father didn't know what to do. I could see in his eyes how uncomfortable he was, and the rest of my family banded together in a tight circle, quiet, confused. Intimidated.

You could feel the Spirit of God hovering over us, engulfing the halls of the house, encircling my family. The power of his presence was palpable.

I made my way to the living room, where my mother was lying on the sofa, and stood about six feet away from her. I can still see her eyes as she looked at me, frightened and confused. She knew who I was; I could tell by her anxious gaze.

The windows were open and a sudden burst of cool east wind blew through the house, through the halls, filling the rooms with freshness. It was as if God's Spirit had burst through the window, cleansing the house of evil, joining us in our rumble against the king of darkness. Everyone felt it. Everyone knew that God's Spirit had come to rest among us, to show his muscle, to shine grace and mercy upon this house of evil, to open the gates of hell and set the captive free.

I noticed the pastor standing across the room from me, and he asked me to say something. I tried to speak, but the words wouldn't come. Tears flooded the sides of my face as I stood weeping, my eyes closed, my heart filled with mixed emotions.

What do I say? I wanted to pray, but the words wouldn't come. My mind was in a fog. Tears grew even thicker on my cheeks as I stood silently before my mother and a room filled with strangers. I wanted so desperately for God to work a miracle in my mother's heart. I knew that he could. He had done such a miracle in my heart and for many others that I knew.

At that instant, Jesus spoke to my heart as clearly as he's ever spoken. *Nicky,* he said, *this is your mother. I know that she hasn't been the mother you needed. I know the pain you feel. But today is the day of forgiveness. I forgave you, Nicky, but now you need to forgive your mother. Let it go.*

As I stood there sobbing, drenched in my own tears, I suddenly felt a tug at the bottom of my pants leg. It shocked me, and I quickly opened my eyes. To this day I don't know how my mother made her way off the sofa and to my feet, but as I looked down I saw her feeble frame on the floor beneath me. She could barely raise her arms, yet she found the strength to reach up for me. Her eyes begged me to touch her, to talk to her.

I dropped to my knees and found myself face to face with my mother. She was still reaching out toward me, her eyes filled with tears. "Nicky," she said, "I know how much I've hurt you. I've destroyed you. I have no right to ask you this, but if you can find it in your heart, please forgive me. I'm so sorry for all I've done."

I tried to speak, but the words wouldn't come. Never had my mother looked at me this way. Never had I seen anything but hate exploding from her eyes, and now she looked at me with love. I couldn't hold back my tears. I looked deep into her eyes, and she spoke again. "Nicky, please let me kiss you."

I leaned my face in closer, and my mother kissed me on the cheek. Her lips were warm and tender—lips that had never before touched my face. Not once in my childhood could I remember her kissing me. I blubbered like a bruised child.

At that very instant I could feel God reach into my heart and take away the pain, the hate, the indifference. For the first time in my life, I loved my mother. The fear was gone. The chasm between us was bridged forever. I felt nothing but love and forgiveness in my heart.

"Mama," I said, "you know I forgive you. I love you."

Our eyes met and she melted in my arms, sobbing even harder. For an eternity we wept in each other's arms. Then I said to her, "Give your heart to Jesus, Mama. He's the one who wants to forgive you. Accept Jesus's love, Mama. You need Jesus!"

There on the floor, crying in my arms, my mother accepted Jesus into her heart. I prayed with her as she asked God to forgive her for a lifetime of hate and sin. With my own eyes I saw the Spirit of God come upon her. Even as I was praying, I could feel her bones strengthen. Her eyes became clear as never before. She rose to her feet before me, still feeble, but able to stand, able to think and speak clearly for the first time in months.

In front of the crowd and my family, not only did God forgive my mother, but he healed her. Though the doctors said she would probably not last through the night, she grew stronger before our eyes. All around people stood clapping, praying, rejoicing at the miracle we had all witnessed. The witch of Las Piedras was now a child of God!

A BROKEN CURSE

My mother lived another twenty-five years and seven months, and she remained faithful to God until her dying day. In that time she was able to bring my father to Jesus. He renounced witchcraft and turned his heart toward God. Hundreds of people throughout the island were impacted by my mother's faith. She developed a passion for Jesus, and her faith became as real and strong as anyone's I have ever known.

Through those years, she and I grew closer than I ever imagined possible. I never again felt anything but love for my mother, and she felt the same for me. Finally I was able to get to know who my mother really was, not the cold mother that I remembered from my past, but who she was in her heart.

God began to reveal to me the pain and confusion that she had lived with all those years. How intimidated she had felt by my father, a strong and stern man, caught up in Satan's evil grip. At a young age he seduced her into a life of witchcraft and sorcery and all that was connected to it, and she spent many years bound alongside him. I've always thought it ironic that she would later free my father from the life that he had drawn her into and that she would introduce him to Jesus.

My mother found herself completely overwhelmed by the task of raising so many children and trying to keep her home together. She wanted so much to be a good mother, to be a loving, caring wife, but she didn't know how. She had married so young and beautiful into a world that she knew nothing about, a world of occultism and witchery and black magic. A world that soon came to consume her.

But God came in and took all that away. He gave us back the years we lost to Satan. He redeemed the days of evil and restored our family forever. Today my only sister and thirteen of my brothers are serving Jesus. Three of them are ministers of the gospel. My family has been securely planted into the Tree of Life forever. No more curse of darkness haunts us. Satan has no more hold on the Cruz family. We once served him, but now we despise him. We are eternally free! And each of us pursues Jesus with a relentless passion!

What I have experienced in my family is a miracle far beyond what I expected when I gave my heart to Jesus. I never imagined he would reach into my past and erase it, breaking the curse that had plagued us for as long as anyone could remember. He did for us what only God can do—what he has done for so many through the years. He took away the pain and replaced it with love. He removed the anger and exchanged it for forgiveness.

Hearts that once cursed him now burn with a holy passion for his love.

Children who grew up in pain and abuse now harbor only mercy and compassion for others. Slaves who once bowed down to Satan now live under a glorious new covenant with God.

A Heart of Purpose

That's how God works when he redeems his people. He does so much more than save us; he *restores* us. Whatever Satan has stolen, God gives back. Whatever time we've lost to sin, he reclaims through love. The wounds inflicted upon us by the world are healed by his wonderful grace.

This is the Jesus we worship—the Savior who died so that we can live!

This is the message we bring to a world still bound by sin.

This is the only testimony worth telling—the only thing that really matters!

How can we not shout it from the rooftops? How can we ever slip into moments of apathy after all that God has done for us? How can we not live with uninhibited passion and zeal, knowing what we know? understanding what we understand about Satan and his lies? after experiencing the unconditional forgiveness that Jesus brings?

How can any man keep silent?

Since the day Jesus came into my heart, my obsession in life has been to save lost souls! At that moment, Jesus burned into my heart a soul obsession—a blazing passion for those in need of a Savior. It is a fire that has never waned, never tired, never relented. It is the blood that runs through my veins—what drives me forward, day after day, month after month, year after glorious year. My heart bursts with the message of God's love and faithfulness, and all I want to do is to share that truth with others!

Someone once asked me, "What is the greatest miracle you've ever seen?" I didn't even have to stop and think before answering. "When God reaches into a heart of sin and replaces it with love—that is God's greatest miracle." I see it happen every day, and each time it is as real and powerful to me as the day I experienced it myself.

People need Jesus, and God wants you and me to lead them toward him. We are the ambassadors of the Holy Spirit, living and working in Satan's playground, and all around us are lost and hurting children, longing to find their way home. There is no greater feeling than taking a child by the hand and leading him into the arms of Jesus. Nothing could possibly compare!

READY FOR SERVICE

But what does it take to do that? What does God need us to do and be in order for him to use us to reach a lost world?

I'm convinced that before any follower of Christ can make a serious impact on humanity, she must exhibit three critical qualities of servanthood. Three character traits that not only allow God to work through us but serve as lightning rods for souls needing salvation.

The first is *passion.* A passion for Jesus and a passion for those who need him. A passion that goes far beyond what the church and the world are accustomed to seeing—beyond mere excitement and into the realm of fanaticism.

The second is *mercy.* A merciful heart is a critical ingredient in the life of a follower. If we can't learn to see people the way Jesus sees them, to love them with the same love he has shown us, to serve them the way Jesus served during his days on earth, to care with the same compassion that drove Jesus to his death on the cross...if we can't develop that kind of mercy, we will never be able to reach a lost and dying world.

The third is *vision*. Each of us needs a covenant with God—a mission, a purpose, a clear sense of our gifts and talents and our true calling in the kingdom. You and I were created with a specific need and assignment in mind, and God has been preparing us to fulfill the mission that he set in place before we were born. But how seldom we seem to find our purpose. How seldom we embrace the vision that God has set before us.

Passion. Mercy. Vision.

Three qualities that should be standard ingredients in the life of every follower. Three traits that every believer needs in order to make a serious impact on the world. Three necessary elements for developing a soul obsession in the depths of your heart!

Stay with me as we explore each of these three elements deeper.

But if from there you seek the LORD your God,
you will find him if you look for him with
all your heart and with all your soul.

DEUTERONOMY 4:29

Come with me and see my zeal for the LORD.

2 KINGS 10:16

Now devote your heart and soul to
seeking the LORD your God.

1 CHRONICLES 22:19

They broke bread in their homes and ate together
with glad and sincere hearts, praising God and enjoying the favor of all the people. And the Lord added to
their number daily those who were being saved.

ACTS 2:46-47

And hope does not disappoint us, because
God has poured out his love into our hearts by
the Holy Spirit, whom he has given us.

ROMANS 5:5

For God, who said, "Let light shine out of darkness,"
made his light shine in our hearts.

2 CORINTHIANS 4:6

PART I: THE PASSION

CHAPTER ONE

NAKED FAITH

L ong before I was able to comprehend the relentless love of God, I felt it. Though I could never quite assimilate it in my mind or grasp it with my understanding, I could sense it in my heart. Still today I struggle to define it, yet it is as real to me as the air I breathe and the water I drink.

This love affair began the day I accepted Jesus into my heart at the age of nineteen, but it didn't really take hold in my spirit until many years later. And it happened in the most unlikely of places.

I was twenty-seven at the time and had been booked to speak at a crusade in Albuquerque, New Mexico. As a young evangelist in the beginning stages of a new speaking ministry, I wasn't yet used to the loneliness of life on the road. It was late at night, and I was staying in a small, dingy motel room that consisted of a bed, a lamp, and a tiny bathroom. Nothing else.

I was in prayer, asking God to give me the words I needed for my sermon the next evening. My normal routine was to read my Bible for a time and then stop and pray that God would speak to me through the words, give me some kind of insight and guidance. I prayed mostly that he would bring to my mind those things I needed to say in order to best minister to the people attending my crusades.

Even though I was young and new to the evangelistic circle, God was using me more mightily than I had ever imagined possible. Everywhere I spoke, waves of people would come forward to receive Jesus as their Savior. Every speaking engagement proved to be more powerful than the last, and in my heart I knew it had nothing to do with me. In fact, my accent was so thick that many who came forward hadn't understood half of what I had said. Still they found themselves under the conviction of the Holy Spirit. It was clear that God was moving before me; only he could bring so many to their knees in repentance. I never once thought otherwise.

As I was praying under the dim light of that tiny hotel room, I suddenly felt God's presence as powerfully as I had ever experienced it. At first I wasn't sure what was happening. A feeling of love and intimacy began to sweep over my spirit. I sensed a closeness to him that transcended anything I had ever felt before. It was as if God had reached out and wrapped his large arms around me, drawing my head to his chest. I could all but feel him holding me, smiling at me, putting his hand over my heart.

I began to cry, softly at first, and then uncontrollably. His nearness was almost too much to take in. At that instant I recognized my complete and total dependence on him. With rivers of tears flooding down my face and sobs heaving from my breast, I cried out, "I love you, God. You are my Lord, my King, my power, my only strength! Without you I am nothing!"

For what seemed an eternity I sat weeping, resting in the arms of God. I was like a child who had crawled into his father's arms, and now I wanted nothing more in life than to be held, nurtured, loved as only a father could.

Nothing else mattered. Nothing could come between us. Everything was exactly as it should be.

I wanted to stay there forever.

BEGINNING OF AN AFFAIR

Throughout my walk with God, he has used times like these to reach down and draw me nearer to his love, strengthening my heart and life, building on the romance that began the moment I gave my heart to him. That day in the hotel room was only one of many times in my life when God showed me how much I needed him—and how very much he cared. I've learned that I can always depend on him, that he is always there for me, even when it seems he isn't. Sometimes *especially* when it seems he isn't.

I've learned through the years to trust God completely with my heart and life, to trust him with my relationships, my marriage, my children, my ministry, my finances, my future. And he has never let me down. Never have I put a care on his shoulders that he couldn't carry. Never have I given him a problem he couldn't fix. Never have I spoken where he wasn't there to listen.

I remember one instance, years ago, when I needed God desperately. Our ministry was still small and struggling financially. We had always worked on a tight, shoestring budget—we still do—but for some reason funds were getting tighter than ever. People were not giving, and what little we had in reserve had completely dried up.

Often we spend more on our crusades than we receive in contributions. We almost always have to pay the difference out of our limited operating capital. We don't cancel when this happens; we trust that God will make up the difference. He always has, and I know he always will.

This particular time, we had just completed a large crusade and were forced to empty our account to pay for the balance on the arena and other expenses. We had only a few hundred dollars left in the bank for payroll and rent and any other needs that might come along. It so happened that we were having our annual board meeting that week. I knew I needed to discuss this problem with our board of directors.

We got together on a Friday afternoon, and I informed them just how dire the situation was. We needed around forty-three thousand dollars by Monday to make our payroll and pay our rent and light bill for the month. That would leave no extra funds, but it would at least see us through the crisis at hand. The staff was already aware of the problem, and many wondered if they'd still have a job by Tuesday. It broke my heart to see them worry.

Several on the board suggested that we get out some emergency letters and phone calls to our larger givers in order to inform them of our need. Maybe one of them would come through for us, we reasoned. Others suggested going to a bank for a loan, but we quickly ruled out that option.

After several hours of discussion, I said to them, "If God wants this ministry to survive, he will come through for us. I'm not going to write any letters and beg for money. God is the only one we need to go to. He's aware of our problem, and that's where we need to leave it. If this is God's ministry, he will give us what we need."

The board agreed, and we spent the remaining time in prayer before disbanding for the weekend.

That evening I went to dinner with the board members and tried to put the problem behind me, but it persisted in my mind. I couldn't seem to feel at peace. I trusted God, but I also felt responsible for my staff. I couldn't bear the thought of letting them go, of disappointing so many of our faithful co-workers, of seeing the ministry fold, of losing what we had worked so hard to build.

I don't always share financial problems with my wife, Gloria, but that evening I told her how desperate things were. I had considered taking out a second mortgage on our home to pay our staff, and I knew I needed to let Gloria know our situation. I wanted to prepare her for the difficult times that could be in our future. We prayed together, and she told me I shouldn't worry. I knew she was right, but still I agonized.

I spent much of that evening in prayer, pleading with God to come through for us, to help me feel at peace, to give me a sign that he is in control. Yet I felt nothing. I listened for God, but no word came. I wondered if he might be angry with me, if maybe our ministry had done something to offend him, yet I couldn't think of anything. I begged him for a sense of his presence, for even a hint of confirmation, yet nothing came. I prayed that Monday would never arrive. I couldn't bear the thought of facing my staff with so much uncertainty in the wind.

I barely slept that night. Much of the next day I put up a good front, but my spirit was deeply concerned. *Why does God feel so distant?* I thought. *Where is he? Why can't I find any peace?* It was one of the most agonizing and introspective days of my life.

A Break in the Cloud

Saturday night, after dinner, I was lying on my sofa in the family room when suddenly I felt a deep urge in my spirit. God was calling me to pray. He wanted me to get alone and talk with him. Without speaking, I jumped from the sofa and ran to our bedroom. Closing the door behind me, I sat on the edge of the bed and began talking to God.

"Sweet Jesus, you know I'm yours. You've always been faithful to me. I have a wonderful life. You've given me Gloria, the best wife any man could have. You've given me four wonderful children. I'm the most blessed man on earth, and nothing that happens can make me forget that truth. But right now I'm confused and tired and worried. There's so much uncertainty in my spirit. I don't know what's going to happen with the ministry—*your* ministry—that you've entrusted me to watch over. Have I done something wrong? Do you have other plans for me? What am I supposed to do, Lord?

"Jesus, I stand before you with nothing but a naked faith. Nothing else. I have no idea what to do, but I trust you completely. Show me the way, Lord, and I promise to follow."

As I sat pouring my soul out to God, I could sense his presence. His peace filled the room and enveloped my spirit. I began to cry as his tenderness overwhelmed me. I could almost feel his heart next to mine. And I listened as he spoke into my spirit.

Nicky, he said, *I know you are caught up in fear, but I have never let you down. I'm not through with you yet. You've done nothing wrong. Nothing is going to happen with your ministry. Trust me.*

For the next hour I sat weeping in the arms of Jesus. I thanked God for his goodness, for giving me a sense of peace, for telling me that everything was going to be all right. I knew that I had no more worries. He would come through for me, just as he always had.

From that moment on my attitude completely changed. I no longer fretted. I slept so well that night that I jumped out of bed early the next morning and couldn't wait to get to church to worship God. Gloria couldn't believe the change in my demeanor. The worry was completely gone. I had no idea how God was going to fix the problem; I just knew that he would. I couldn't wait for Monday to see what God would do.

WAITING FOR A MIRACLE

I can still remember the sense of uneasiness among the staff when I walked into the office Monday morning. I could tell they had all spent a weekend of worry, and I tried my best to calm their fears. "Don't worry," I told them. "God will come through for us. You'll see."

I couldn't explain my sense of comfort, but I had absolutely no doubt that God would fix our financial problem. I didn't know how he would do it; I just knew that he would. We had never received forty-three thousand dollars in contributions in one day, and we all were aware of that fact. Most of our funds came in through small contributors who were far from wealthy but helped us with ten, twenty, or fifty dollars whenever they could. God would have to work a mighty miracle for us to be able to continue our work. I felt badly that my staff was so concerned, but my spirit was completely at ease.

The mail almost always came at noon, but this day it was late. I remember my secretary checking the window every fifteen minutes, watching for the mailman. Two o'clock rolled around, yet still he hadn't come.

Just before three, my secretary walked into my office with tears running down her face. The mail had just come, and the staff quickly opened it. She held in her hands two checks. Both were from large contributors whom we hadn't heard from in some time. The checks totaled fifty-seven thousand dollars.

Both envelopes came with nothing but simple notes inside explaining that God had put it on their hearts to send us a check.

I gathered my staff into my office and we said a short prayer, thanking God for bringing such a wonderful gift. He had given us even more than we needed.

A God of Guts

God has a way of taking our moments of deepest confusion and doubt and using them to strengthen our trust and dependence on him. He takes our seeds of faith and turns them into a tower of conviction and confidence. When we are most perplexed, he is most in control. When we are weakest, he is strongest. When we need him, he is always there.

David Wilkerson, my friend and mentor, is a living testament to this truth. More than any man I know, he trusts God implicitly. He never allows confusion or doubt or other people to steer his decisions. Every worry, every question, every moment of concern is placed at the feet of Jesus until he hears an answer. He listens to God and God alone. That's why God has used him so mightily in his life and ministry.

David Wilkerson was just a country preacher from Pennsylvania when God spoke to him and told him to go to New York and reach out to the gangs. He had been watching a news program that discussed the rampant gang problem in the inner city when God spoke to his spirit and told him to go. No one could imagine this skinny preacher being able to reach such a hardened group, yet he obeyed and went.

I'll never forget his boldness in the face of such danger. He stood alone on the street corner and talked about Jesus with nothing but a Bible in his hand while we laughed and taunted him. I was only nineteen at the time and a warlord of the Mau Maus, the most brutal and notorious gang in the city. None of us could believe this strange little man dared to venture onto our turf to tell us about God. Any one of us could have cut him to shreds without losing a moment's sleep over it. We were convinced that he was crazy, that he had no idea how much danger he was in, that he would never have come if he had known how little we respected human life.

But we were wrong. Not only did he understand the danger, he welcomed it. He had no fear, no worry, no doubt that God would protect him. God called him to reach out to us, so he came and stood three inches from hell and threw his fishing line over the edge, laughing at the devil every step of the way. Wilkerson trusted God completely, and nothing we could do intimidated him.

We hurt him, cursed at him, humiliated him, screamed in his face, yet he kept coming back. Wilkerson's courage in the face of danger was the one thing that intrigued me enough to attend his service. I would never have stepped foot into a church building had I not been so fascinated by his guts, his complete disregard for his own safety. *What would make a man do such a thing? What kind of God would give a man such confidence, such trust, such gumption that he could walk into the middle of hell and stare down the devil himself? What would make a skinny street preacher think he could come onto our turf and tell us what to believe?*

I had to know, so I went to his service. And that's when God grabbed hold of my heart.

There, in the middle of St. Nicholas Arena, in front of hundreds of strangers and dozens of my fellow gang members, I fell to my knees before the altar and surrendered. I bawled like a baby in front of my friends. I cried out for Jesus to save me, and he did. I gave up trying to do it on my own. I looked at David Wilkerson, at the love in his eyes, at the peace in his spirit, at the courage in his heart, and I knew that I wanted what he had. This was a God I could worship. This was a Jesus I could relate to.

This is the kind of faith that I want to live with—that I want to be willing to die for!

Living a Naked Faith

So many people think that my passion for Jesus comes from years of study and prayer and ministry, but they are wrong. It comes from seeing God come through for me during those times when life has left me completely exposed and alone. It comes from feeling God's presence during moments of my greatest confusion and despair. It comes from seeing God's hand before me, time and time again, in the face of unimaginable danger.

Every time I stand face to face with a hardened, teenage gangbanger, I see Wilkerson fearlessly preaching on the corner of my street. Every time I walk into the middle of a crime-ridden, drug-infested neighborhood, I feel the same strength that drove Wilkerson to the streets of New York so many years ago. Every time I hold a lost and hurting soul in my arms, I feel God's power and presence.

I depend only on God. God has used the pain of my past to take me to a deeper level, to bring me closer to him. What Satan intended for evil, God has used for his glory. Any joy I receive in life pales in comparison to the ecstasy of seeing God accomplish the impossible, watching how he reaches into a dark heart and brings light, how he spreads his mercy like butter across the sins of those who need forgiveness.

It's so easy to intellectualize God, to acknowledge his power without ever experiencing it, to believe in his supremacy without ever calling on him to do mighty things in our presence. We see him with our minds but not our hearts. We never embrace the power that we preach to be true. We never call on God to move mightily in our presence—to take our ounce of faith and use it to lift a mountain off of its pedestal and hurl it to the bottom of the sea!

Naked faith demands that we somehow learn to marry the mind and the spirit. That we put away our pride and doubt and fear and stand before God, empty and broken, with nothing but a raw and unquenchable trust. That we close our eyes and ears to the voices that tell us what God can and can't do, what God does and doesn't believe, how God does and doesn't work, and allow God to show us for himself.

God wants us to move past our doubts, to crush our fears, to forget the natural and move instead into the world of the supernatural. Stand on this truth, believe this truth, embrace this truth, and you will see miracles! You won't see God, but you will feel him. You can't brush his robe, but you can smell him as he passes in front of you. You can't touch his face, but you can experience his power.

You can't see him with your mind, but you can see him with your heart.

My trust is often blind but never irrational. It seldom makes sense but always brings results. It can't always be explained, but it always feels right.

If I had one message to shout from the rooftop of every church building on the planet, it would be this:

God is bigger than your doubt!

No matter how grim things look, no matter how much pain you feel, no matter how confused and tired you may be, trust him. He will take your naked faith, no matter how small, and create a miracle bigger than you've ever dreamed or imagined.

CHAPTER TWO

STOLEN PASSION

I've always hesitated to talk much about my father. I'm not sure why. I suppose it's because I've struggled so hard to understand him. I've written more than fifteen books, but in these books there's almost nothing about him. People know from my past that he was a warlock and a spiritist, a follower of the occult. I've written that he was a stern man, a strong man, a firm disciplinarian. And yet people know so little about who he really was, his many personalities, his tender side, because I've spent almost no time writing or speaking about him.

I never called my father Dad or Papa or Father. I called him Don Galo. All of his children did. It was a term of respect and admiration—a name you give someone you admire but fear.

My father was such a hard man to get a handle on. And the memories I have are often confusing and disjointed. I grew up with him, and even I don't completely understand who he really was. What was in his mind and heart and spirit. He never let me close enough to find out. Satan kept him at arm's length, kept his mind confused, kept his heart buried beneath a pile of lies and deceit and evil.

THE SEDUCTION OF EVIL

The power that Satan gave my father can't be denied. Everyone who knew him was amazed at his ability to heal or to summon strength from his black magic. It was the thing I most feared about him.

One of my earliest memories of this still haunts me. I don't know how young I was, only that I was at least old enough to remember the event.

My father came into the house one day tired, exhausted from whatever he had been doing. The strength was completely gone from his bones, and he walked slowly, hunched over. He moved to the sofa and lay down to rest. He instructed us to leave him alone, that he needed to sleep, so we did.

All day my father lay on the couch, stiff and lifeless. He never once turned over. His body looked pale and rigid. Mother kept telling us to be quiet as we went through the room, and we obeyed her. Mostly because we were afraid of what he might do if we woke him up.

He lay there all day and into the night, and he was still rigid and motionless the next morning. At one point I wondered if he was still alive. I'd never seen him in such a deep, deep sleep. Almost like a coma.

Late that evening, for no apparent reason, my father suddenly woke up. He sat up on the sofa and stared straight ahead for several minutes. Then he jumped to his feet, completely reenergized. He was wide-awake and fresh. I remember him looking around the room and smiling, pacing back and forth, as if he were filled with pent-up energy just waiting to burst out of his chest. It was good to see my father so happy. He always seemed so stressed and tired, and now he was like a little kid—vibrant and well rested. Yet something about his eyes still frightened me.

All at once he walked over to the corner of the room and placed his hands on the wall of our small wooden house. I can't remember how many of us kids were in the room, only that Mama was there, along with several of my brothers. I stayed to one side, trying not to draw attention to myself.

"I want you to watch this," my father said to us. "I'm going to shake this house!" His voice was loud and confident, almost defiant.

He stood with his hands on the house and his gaze cast upward, like he was concentrating—maybe even praying. And at that moment the house began to shake, just a little at first, then escalating into a full rumble. I felt the earth vibrate beneath my feet. The house shook from its very foundation. For several seconds we stood immobilized, afraid to move, feeling our bodies shiver from the quake. Then it stopped as quickly as it had started.

My father removed his hand from the wall and gazed around the room, looking at us one by one. He said nothing, just stared and smiled. My mother looked terrified. I can still see the terror in her eyes as she looked at my father. Even she was taken back by this display of power—this unmistakable force that coursed through my father's veins.

From that moment on, I never once doubted the reality of my father's witchcraft. The power it gave him. The strength that he could summon from his strange and elusive spirits.

DABBLING IN DANGER

People wonder why I am so opposed to children dabbling in occultist games and practices. Teenagers think it's fun to play fantasy games, like

Dungeons and Dragons, where they pretend to be different characters and spirits. These types of games encourage them to call on these spiritual entities for strength and power and protection. And teens—even Christian teens—dabble in these games as if they are harmless pastimes, as if they are some kind of candy. But what these kids are doing is far from harmless. And it amazes me that parents allow them to play.

If they could see what I've seen, experience what I've experienced, feel just a sampling of the fear that I lived with as a child, they would never again take these magic arts so lightly. They would know how dangerous and real and intoxicating such practices can be. How quickly Satan can use them to draw innocent lives into his evil lair.

As a spiritist, my father drank of this power, craved it, displayed it, worshiped it in his heart. And it completely consumed his life.

Because of this spiritual influence, my father was a confused man. He so easily became angered and didn't know how to control his fierce temper. He was a stern disciplinarian, but his discipline often went too far. He would spank us furiously, relentlessly, usually more out of rage than correction. Today his discipline would be considered child abuse, but to him it was simply a way of keeping his children in line.

As a child I adored my father, but I also feared him greatly. I loved him, but I hated his temper. I saw his anger flare so often, but I also saw a tender side to him. A side that many never got to see. A side that still brings tears to my eyes when I reflect on my childhood.

My father was terribly harsh, but he could also be loving and vulnerable. Somewhere, deep inside, deep beneath the cobwebs that Satan had woven throughout the walls of his heart, deep beneath the anger and hostility and evil, somewhere beneath all that, my father was a good man. An honorable man. A loving and caring man. A man who wanted so much to be a good husband and father. A man who longed to find God, though he never knew how.

With every fiber of my being, I hate Satan for what he did to my parents.

A Sobering Memory

I remember walking along the long road leading away from my parents' house. I was seven at the time, on my way to the center of Las Piedras, about a five-minute walk from our home. I was looking for my father.

I found him in a bar. He was never a heavy drinker, but he enjoyed an occasional glass of wine or beer. This day, for some reason, he was drinking rum. I looked through the window and saw him throw back a large swig, and the scene shocked me.

He was with three other men, talking and drinking. I saw him turn to the man on his right and gesture widely with his hands, as if to say to the man, "It's over. Don't worry about it." Somehow I knew that something had gone on between them. Maybe the man had offended him or argued or worse. And now my father was telling him that the matter was over. Forgotten. He was through arguing about it.

As I stood watching him, I noticed him sway and stagger. Immediately I knew he was drunk, and I had never seen my father drunk. Never had I seen him drink so much that he stumbled. Even today I shiver as I think back to the sight.

The scene frightened me, confused me. I wanted to go in and get him, take the bottle from his hands, put it on the counter, and take him home with me. I wanted him to stop drinking and leave, to come home with me to see Mama. But I didn't want to make him angry, so I just stood and watched. Watched as he drank one swig after another with his friends.

For two solid hours I stood and watched my father through the window. I felt like a little puppy tied to a post, waiting for his master to come and take him home. It was a helpless, hopeless feeling. A weak feeling.

Finally my father stood up from his barstool. He stumbled and fell against the bar. He tried to walk, but each time he fell against the rail. I ran in the door and over to his side. I could tell he was surprised to see me. "Let me help you, Don Galo," I said. "Let me take you home."

I wrapped his large, powerful arm around my neck and grabbed him around the waist, using all my strength to help him to his feet. He was so strong and heavy and hard to lift. The muscles in his forearm cut into the base of my neck as we walked. He tried to talk, but I couldn't understand what he was saying. "I'll get you home, Don Galo. Just hang onto me."

With all the strength I could muster, I got him out the front door and down the steps of the bar. The road to our house looked so long, and my father was getting heavier by the minute. I wondered if I'd be able to make it. But I couldn't stop. Couldn't leave him in town. Couldn't let any more people see him in this condition. One step at a time we worked our way home. I cried as I walked. Partly because of the pain, but mostly because I was embarrassed for my father. I hated to see him like this. And I knew, even at my young age, how it broke his heart for me to see it.

At one point the weight of his body became too great and I fell. I landed with one knee digging into the sharp rocks of the road and the other in a patch of prickly plants. The fall sliced my leg in several places. I cried even harder.

Again I summoned the strength to stand and take a few more steps, his large frame still draped across my small body. A few feet later we fell again. Then again. And again. But always I made my way back to my feet. So many times we fell along the way, and each time I cut and bruised myself further. The pain was tremendous, but I had to get my father home. Had to get him into bed, so he could sleep off his liquor. Had to get him away from the eyes of the village gossips.

I don't know how long it took us to get home, only that I was completely exhausted when we arrived. My legs were red and black with blood and scrapes and dirt. I was in such pain. But we were home, and my father was safely in bed.

The next day my father woke completely sober. I've never seen him so embarrassed and repentant as he was when he saw me that morning. He looked like a beaten dog, ashamed, cowering. He ran his hands along the scrapes and bruises on my leg, then said to me, "I'm so sorry, Nicky. I'm sorry you had to do that. I will never get drunk like that again. I promise. You will never see me that way again."

And I never did. He stayed true to that promise.

REVEALING HIS TRUE HEART

This memory is still fresh in my mind for many reasons. First, because I hurt so bad for my father. It hurt me to see him so helpless and ashamed and weak. That's not the way that I remember him—not the way that I *want* to remember him. Because that's not who he was.

And second, because it showed me a side of him that I so seldom got to see. A tender side. A remorseful side. A caring side. He hurt so deeply for me. Not just because of the cuts and bruises, but because I had to see him in such a weak and vulnerable condition. Because I would live with that memory for the rest of my life. And down deep, I think he feared that this memory would define how I remembered him.

But that's not what it did. This memory doesn't define him for me; it explains him. In a strange way it has become for me a small and brief glimpse into his true heart. Something of a testament to what I've always wanted to believe was true about my father. That down deep, deep in the crevices of his soul, he wasn't a powerful warlock or some mighty witch doctor; he was a gentle, frightened little boy. An honorable, vulnerable, caring person. A confused man, caught in a world so seductive and evil that he didn't know how to escape.

I recoil at this memory, but I cherish it. Because within it lies the truth behind my father's cold and hard eyes.

STOLEN YEARS

When my father left this world, he went out singing the praises of Jesus. Late in his life he renounced witchcraft, renounced Satan, and accepted Jesus as his Lord and Savior. My mother brought him to the Lord before his death, and now the two of them are together in heaven, dancing along the golden streets, basking in God's glory, relishing their new eternal home with God. When I close my eyes, I can almost hear them shouting out in worship to their new King. Their Savior. Their glorious Redeemer!

How I wish my father could have enjoyed such a life on earth. I would give anything to have seen him worship God on earth as passionately as he served Satan. He would have been such an effective witness, such a powerful evangelist, such a great and mighty preacher of God's Word.

Everything he did, he did with passion. His faith would have been so real and strong and unquenchable. He would have commanded such great miracles. He would have trusted God completely, drunk of his Word, followed him wherever he might lead! His heart would have burned with a soul obsession! Because that's the kind of man he was.

Instead of cowering before the devil, he could have spent his life hurting him, defeating him, bruising him. He could have had such an impact on the world. If only my father could have found Jesus at an early age.

Don't let Satan steal your life and heart the way he stole my father's. Don't be seduced by his lies. Don't be taken in by his charm or led astray by his empty promises. Put your faith in Jesus. Give your life to one who wants to lift you up, not tear you down. The one who loves and cares for you. The one who brings true power and strength, not puny parlor tricks.

As a man, my father was able to shake his house through the power of Satan. But with God he could have sent a quake that shook the very foundations of the world.

Don't let Satan rob you the way he robbed my father. Don't let him blind you to the truth of God's goodness. Let Jesus be the power in your hands. Put your trust in an extraordinary God!

CHAPTER THREE

FIRE IN NORWAY

P eople are surprised when I tell them of the large Muslim population in Europe. Most Americans don't realize how quickly the religion is growing overseas and how many young people are buying into the Muslim faith. But the problem is very real, especially in the European arena.

In 2003 there were more than two million Muslims in Britain alone, and it is predicted that soon Muslims will outnumber Anglicans. Muslims are immigrating in record numbers and having a large number of children. English women are marrying Muslim men and converting to their faith. Today Muslims are involved in the educational system and have members at all levels of the government. They've formed their own political party and regularly put on exhibitions in schools and public functions. Muslim leaders in Britain have made no secret of their plans to soon take the United Kingdom for Islam, and they are very close to accomplishing that goal.

One of the largest churches in England is an African American church that has been trying for years to buy property to expand, yet they continue to be denied by the government and local officials. Muslims are in control within the seats of power in their community, and they are purposely targeting this church for persecution.

The worst part is, they've been able to create a climate of fear. It's unacceptable to criticize Islam, although Christianity is under constant fire and mocked openly.

Fred Markert, director of Youth With a Mission (YWAM) in the United States, often says that we are in the midst of the third great Islamic resurgence, and Europe is considered the front line of this battle. It is a well-planned step in their long-range strategy of taking the entire world for Islam—including the United States.

Some studies show that today more than seven million Muslims live in France alone. By 2040 it is predicted that more than 55 percent of Europe will be Muslim (and if this trend holds true, by 2055 the number will be 75 percent). And let's not forget the United States. The Muslim population has steadily increased in the States for years, and now Islam is officially the second largest religion, even passing Judaism!

A large number of Islamic families in the Middle East send their children to school in Europe. Not only do the children get a good education, but their parents know their kids won't be swayed by Christianity. Followers of Christ in Europe are not as much a threat to them as they should be, and there are lots of Muslim mosques to attend—more than two thousand in the United Kingdom alone, many of which are former pubs, cinemas, and churches! This is why mosques are thriving all over Europe, especially in the Scandinavian regions.

The more statistics you hear, the more alarmed you become. As a believer, it's shocking to see how much ground the Muslims have been able to gain and how quickly they are still growing. And they are doing so by targeting young people.

Muslims understand that today more than half of the world's population is under the age of twenty-four, so they capitalize on that fact. They target the youth, because the youth are our future. And young people are an easy target, because so many are turned off to Christianity. The Christian faith is seen as an old religion, a part of the past, and many young people have systematically rejected everything that is considered old and past.

That's why our ministry has been so intent on reaching young people for Jesus. We know the real message that Christ brings to the world, and there is nothing old or outdated about it. It is real and relevant and life-changing. Muslims claim that their religion brings holiness, modesty, and virtue, but it brings only oppression and force. We know that holiness and virtue are not traits you can force on someone. Only the Holy Spirit can bring about such a transformation. Only Jesus can change your heart. And only God can save you. This is the message that Jesus brought, and this is the message we bring to young people around the world.

We can't stop the flood of Muslims moving into Europe and the Western world. We can't stop them from having babies and proselytizing their false religion. But we can answer their lies about the Christian faith with the truth! We can begin to give a true picture of who Jesus is and what he stands for. We can bring the good news the way it was meant to be brought—not through fear but through love.

And we can begin by targeting those who have rejected our message. The youth. That half of the world's population under the age of twenty-four—the group that the Muslims have been successfully targeting with their lies.

I'm convinced that a revival will happen, and it will begin with the youth of the world. The Holy Spirit is already moving among the youth of Latin America and Africa, and the revival will continue to spread worldwide.

Young people don't want to hear about theology; they want to see God in action. They are saying, "I want to see if God is who he says he is!" And God is answering their cries. They are seeing God do great miracles in their midst, because they know in their hearts that he can. The dead are being raised, mountains are being moved, and lives are being transformed because of their childlike faith.

If Europe is to be reclaimed for Jesus, it will happen through a youth revival because youth represent the future of Europe. Bring them to Jesus, and they will bring Jesus to the European world. Because young people understand the boldness of Satan, they will attack with the boldness of God!

CALLED TO NORWAY

In the summer of 2002, God called our ministry to plan an evangelistic outreach in Norway, in the city of Oslo. At the time we were confused by this leading of the Spirit, because I had never considered this region as part of God's vision for our ministry. I've spoken all over Europe and was well aware of how much the gospel is needed, yet I had never considered Oslo as a unique or prime target for our brand of ministry. Still, God was very clear, so we set our plans in motion. Only later did we understand why.

During our outreach to Norway, I left briefly to tour Germany and Austria. While I was there a minister asked me why I was wasting my time in Norway—a country with fewer than four and a half million people. He thought I should be spending my energies on places where people spoke English and Spanish. I was offended by his comment and told him that I go wherever God leads me. I've always thought it was shortsighted and prejudiced to bypass a nation because of language barriers. This experience did nothing more than reconfirm that God had called us to Norway.

Europeans are very quiet, private people, and it takes them a while to be comfortable enough to share their faith with others. They love the Lord; they just tend to be more uncomfortable proselytizing. In many circles it is considered rude and socially unacceptable to talk about your faith in public.

It didn't take them long to realize in Oslo that Nicky Cruz Outreach isn't worried much about European social graces. They might as well ask the sun not to rise in the east as to expect us to keep our faith a secret! We hit the streets with a vengeance and immediately began to make our mark.

Our Twelve Disciples

Our crusades are anchored by a group of ten to twelve young people, musicians and dancers who travel with us wherever we go. We call them our Twelve Disciples (though the number varies). They are trained at our TRUCE Evangelistic Training Center in New York. The youngest is about seventeen, and the oldest, a man named David, is in his late twenties. David is the director of TRUCE and the training center. He's a powerful musician and a natural leader.

These kids are some of the most gifted performers I've worked with, and each one has a fire for the Lord burning in his heart—a soul obsession that will never be quenched. They are the most passionate young people you can find—passionate about God and grateful for what he has done in their lives. Most of them come from homes of abuse and neglect and drugs, homes in the inner cities and ghettos of America.

One young girl was raised in a terribly dysfunctional house—a house torn apart by drugs, alcohol, and divorce. Her father abused her as a child, and as a young teen she tried to take her life, but thankfully she didn't succeed. She lived and soon found Jesus, and it changed her future forever. As one of our backup singers, she has become a powerful witness for Jesus, both on and off the stage.

Another young man is from Brooklyn, from a home of complete poverty. As a child he never knew if food would be on the table when he woke in the morning. His parents were addicts who would leave the children alone for days at a time. His stories of abuse and neglect would bring tears to your eyes, yet today he is one of our most potent disciples. You'd be hard pressed to find a bolder witness for Jesus. Though he is small and skinny, I've watched him stare down some of the most dangerous looking gangbangers on the street. He stands before them with no fear, no reserve, telling them about Jesus and the forgiveness that he brings.

I wish you could see what I've seen from this handful of ragtag kids from the ghetto. God has taken them by the heart and is using them mightily for his purposes. And each time we witness, their faith grows even stronger.

In the Streets of Oslo

We call our roving street events Hit 'n' Runs. And it was clear from the first moment that the people of Oslo had never seen anything quite like it. We would take our group of Twelve Disciples, along with about forty to one hundred volunteers from the area, and set up a stage on a street corner, complete with microphones and loudspeakers. The music would start and the workers would fan out through the neighborhood, inviting residents to attend our free street concert. Before long, hundreds would flood to the area, most simply curious about all the commotion.

Europeans are fascinated by America's hip-hop culture, and most listen to rap music regularly on the radio, so our brand of music quickly got their attention. But the lyrics were far from what they expected. Our singers don't sing of gangs and drugs and sex; they rap about Jesus and his salvation. Each song is a spiritual testimony put to music.

During one Hit 'n' Run outreach in Oslo, I stood to one side and watched as several hundred Europeans flocked toward the makeshift stage. Most were young people, good-looking kids, well groomed and athletic.

I noticed a young couple standing on the perimeter, watching from a distance. They didn't speak, but simply stood and listened to the music. A worker tried to talk to them, but they politely waved him off and took a few steps back. We gave them their space to see what would happen. A few minutes later I looked up and noticed that they were gone. I wished we had been bolder.

But within about fifteen minutes they had returned. Again they stood on the perimeter, in the same spot they had been before. One of our young women went over to talk with them. "Can I pray for you?" she asked.

"No, that's okay," they told her. "We just want to watch."

She persisted. "Weren't you here a few minutes ago?"

"Yes," they told her.

"I'm curious...why did you come back?" she asked.

Somewhat sheepishly the man answered, "Because we feel something special here. We left and didn't feel it anymore, so we wanted to come back and see what it was."

What the couple felt is what we all feel every time we set up on a street corner. It is the presence of God. The power of the Holy Spirit hovering over the neighborhood, helping us, empowering us, drawing people to himself. It's something we've never been able to describe yet have always been able to feel. You can sense God's nearness, taste it, smell it, feel it in your bones.

There are times when I wish God would show us what is going on in the spiritual realm during our Hit 'n' Run events. Like Elisha, I'd like to ask God to open our eyes and let us see the horses and chariots in the sky, the mighty angels watching over us, protecting us from harm, helping us in our hour of need (see 2 Kings 6:17).

This battle we fight at every turn is very real and palpable. At times I can almost hear the swords and spears flailing in the spiritual realm as God's army keeps the Enemy at bay. Satan's puny troops are no match for the angels of war that God brings to every crusade we plan. The empowerment we feel is often overwhelming and always inspiring.

That's what we feel when we take the gospel of Jesus to the streets. That's what keeps our kids on fire for the Lord. That's the power we experience each and every time—the power that is impossible to adequately explain with words.

Jesus Takes on Islam

God's power is just one of the many differences between our God and the god Muslims serve.

Just days into our ministry in Norway, it became clear why God had called us to the streets of Oslo. We had no idea how many Muslims we would encounter in our mission. From the first time we set up on a street corner, the Muslim teens began coming out of the woodwork. They taunted us, jeered at us, prayed against us, followed us, cursed us insistently. The hate in their hearts was as real as the anger on their lips.

"What are you doing here?" they would ask us. "Your God is weak, and you're not welcome here. Go home to America." Most of what they said shouldn't be repeated in public, but their disdain was clear.

We knew how futile it would be to argue, so we quickly told our workers to abstain from it. I encouraged them to simply respond in love and let God do the rest.

I remember one street event that attracted about a dozen Muslim teenagers. They stood in front of the stage and tried to disrupt the music. Our group continued to sing, but it was all they could do to carry on over the commotion. Afterward several made a point of inviting the Muslims to a large final outreach we would be having at a nearby coliseum. The Muslim teens threw their tracts on the ground and stomped on them. They shouted in our faces, "We hate you, and we hate your God! Go back to America, you dogs!"

It was a brutal confrontation and easily could have turned violent, but our kids never backed away. "I understand," said one boy, "but we love you. And Jesus loves you."

No matter how many times the Muslims flared up in anger, our teens answered with kindness and humility. And each time it diffused the situation entirely. Some angry teenagers would simply storm off down the street, while others would become calm and composed. Many wanted to hear what we had to say about Jesus, so we told them. Even I was surprised at how many would eventually want us to pray with them. It was clear that God was working in their hearts.

And so many of them heeded that call.

AN UNEXPECTED ALLY

During one of our first meetings, we noticed an athletic, good-looking kid hanging around, wanting to see what was going on. He was dark-skinned, obviously from somewhere in the Middle East, and many of the people on the street seemed to know him.

One of the few churches that signed on to help us in our crusade was a large Lutheran fellowship in the inner city. They were an enormous help to us and even allowed our kids to stay in their church building. The volunteer workers they provided were invaluable to the success of our campaign.

This church had set up something of a youth center in its building. They owned an entire city block, and kids on the streets would hang out in their center, playing games and taking dance lessons in the summer. This young man had been coming to the center to dance, and he was curious to see what we were up to. We noticed him watching us each time we met, and then we saw him show up at a few of our street events.

During one of our street outreaches, he began to dance to the music. He was a break dancer, extremely gifted, and the crowd loved watching him. Soon he was showing up at nearly all of our events. Our kids took him under their wings and tried to get to know him, but he seemed elusive, distant. It was all we could do to get him to tell us his first name.

Our kids told me that the boy was really struggling internally. He was quiet, but he asked a lot of questions. People on the street knew him as a partier, a kid who spent much of his time at bars and nightclubs, maybe even into drugs. But our message compelled him, and he kept coming. We prayed for him—and prayed with him—yet he never seemed to respond.

Then one day, several weeks into our outreach, he broke down and started to cry. It was the first time we had seen any emotion from him, and now the tears wouldn't stop. Several of our kids embraced him and prayed with him, and he accepted Jesus into his heart. It was a touching experience—both for him and our workers.

After that he began bringing his friends to our street outreaches several times a week. He asked if he could start coming with us on our street outreaches, and we gladly agreed. He became one of our most diligent evangelists on the streets and stayed with us throughout our time there.

It wasn't until after our time in Oslo that we learned who this kid really was. He was the son of an ambassador from a Middle Eastern country—one of the most influential Muslim leaders in the region. Who knows what impact this young man's conversion to Christ could have on the Muslim world? I'm convinced that God has big plans in store for this boy and his family.

GOD COMES TO OSLO

At the beginning of our outreach to Oslo, our street crusades were attracting between 150 and 200 people each night, but the crowds grew larger as we went. Soon we were attracting 300, then 400, even up to a 1,000.

As usual, we ended each of our street outreaches by passing out invitations to a large, final event to be held at the end of our time there. In Norway this final event was held at the Spektrum, the largest concert venue in the country.

More than five thousand people came the night of our final crusade. The stadium was filled. And these weren't Christians in attendance—the vast majority were unchurched skeptics and hardened cynics. Many of them were Muslims. Even I was surprised to see so many Islamic followers attend a meeting about Jesus. Only God could have gotten them there.

Some of the Christian leaders in Norway were excited about our plans, but a few were apprehensive. Before our group went onto the stage, a couple of the Norwegian Christians took us aside to talk with us. They were concerned about our methods. "If you do an altar call, don't expect a big response like you get in the U.S.," one man told us. "People here aren't really used to that sort of thing."

We politely listened to their advice and then assured them that we were prepared for whatever the Lord chose to do. We knew that where God is involved, anything can happen. When the Holy Spirit is in control, you can never predict what he's going to do.

That night marked one of the most powerful outreaches we have ever been involved with. The Spirit of God was present as powerfully as I've ever witnessed. At the end of the meeting, I gave my testimony and then invited people to come down to the front to accept Jesus as their Savior. No one was prepared for the response we would get—not from this type of audience.

From every corner of the stadium, people flooded the aisles to make their way forward. Hundreds came forward, and many of them were Muslim families. They were weeping and begging for prayer, wanting to accept Jesus as their Savior. The Christians from Norway couldn't believe their eyes. Never had they seen such an outpouring of emotion—not from Europeans, and especially not from Muslims.

Islamic men seldom cry or show any emotion, yet everywhere I looked, these Middle Eastern men were bringing their families forward with tears streaming from their eyes. So many came that we struggled to find room for them all. We didn't have enough workers to pray for everyone, so we had to pray for them in groups of ten or fifteen. I lost count of the number of families I prayed with.

I remember one Muslim family that gathered in a circle to one side, weeping and holding each other tightly. I prayed with them, and later the father threw his arms around me and kissed me on the cheek. It was completely out of character for an Islamic man to do such a thing—to show such unbridled emotion to a foreigner. But then nothing about this evening was characteristic. When God does business with people, all you can do is hang on and try to keep up.

A Hindu doctor also came forward with his entire family. I prayed with them, then introduced them to a Norwegian pastor. He invited them to his church, and the following Sunday they all showed up for worship. They have since become regular and faithful members. I've known the pastor of this church for many years. He once served as my interpreter.

Of the people who came forward, we were only able to reach about eight hundred to receive Christ, though we know many more responded. By the end of the evening our workers were exhausted. The Europeans told us they had never experienced anything like it. God was doing a mighty work in Norway, and we were just thrilled to be a part of it.

News reporters were there from all over the region to report on our crusade, and we woke the next morning to see a front-page headline in *Norway Today*, the nation's largest Christian newspaper. In large bold letters it read, "God Visited Oslo and the Churches Missed It."

The story reported the event as one of the most powerful outpourings of faith ever witnessed in Norway. Reading it for the first time made it clearer than ever why God called us to reach out to Oslo.

Finding Your Fire

Recent studies have predicted that by the year 2020 Islam will be the primary religion in Norway and all Scandinavian countries. If they are right, we can expect to see it as the state religion in Norway within the next fifteen or twenty years. That's what has happened in every other country where Muslims developed a foothold.

It saddens me to see how little impact Christians have been making in

Europe. We've been all but powerless in effectively reaching the lost—not only in European countries but in the United States as well. We pray for God to expand our territory, to help the body of Christ grow and flourish, yet so few denominations are seeing that happen. Most are shrinking, and some are dying out altogether.

What will it take for God to finally grab hold and bring about the transformation we need—the transformation we pray for? When will we finally rise up and make a serious dent in Satan's foothold on the world?

The answer is so simple it feels strange to have to say it: we must trust in God for great miracles! We must rise together with contrite hearts and bold faith, asking God to make us mighty warriors for the kingdom. Like the kids who work with us—our Twelve Disciples—we must open our hearts and lives to God and allow him to instill his passion for souls within us, to develop in our hearts a soul obsession. To break us, to use us, to empower us for service!

When you look at this small band of young people, these twelve unlikely heroes, these bruised and battered kids who own little more than a few sets of clothes and a raging fire of passion in their hearts, and you see how mightily God is using them on the front lines of battle, you begin to get just a small glimpse of what God can do with even the smallest ounce of faith. You suddenly see what it was that caused the early church to explode in numbers, drawing thousands to the faith from only a handful of disciples. You understand what it was that so attracted people to their message—the message of Jesus.

You see how much God can accomplish with so very little.

CHAPTER FOUR

THE DUNGEON OF NOTHINGNESS

Whether we believe it or not, Satan is on a mission. It's a mission that is as simple as it is single-minded. And he is determined to accomplish it.

He is out to steal our passion.

Imagine how effective he can be if he can carry out this one task—this one pursuit. This one thing he desperately needs to achieve. If he can steal our passion, take away our excitement for Jesus, keep us from getting caught up in thoughts of winning souls and reaching the world for Christ, he can effectively keep his dominion on earth intact. He knows that truth, and he works with every fiber of his being to see it happen.

In far too many ways he is succeeding.

Life Inside the Dungeon

Few understand as I do what it means to live a life of hopelessness and despair, a life void of even a hint of passion. A life without Jesus. The first nineteen years of my life were a living hell. Satan had me so bound, so blind, so lost that every moment was simply another fight for survival. I lived like an animal on the streets. I loved no one, wanted no one, cared only for those who could help me survive another day.

My existence was as meaningless as a cockroach in a dark corner. Even today I'm not sure why I didn't just take my own life at a young age. Before I found Jesus, I had no reason to live, no reason to take another breath. No reason to exist.

I remember once hiding behind the corner of a building in the ghettos of New York. I was nineteen at the time and warlord of the Mau Maus, the most dangerous gang in the city. It was three in the morning, and I was stalking a man in an expensive suit—a man who seemed to be begging to be robbed.

I'd seen him around the neighborhood several times. Like a lot of young married men, he had come to our turf to cheat on his wife. Hookers in Brooklyn were cheap and quick and left no emotional attachments. *He's just a rich slime ball,* I thought. *He deserves whatever he gets.* I figured that a man stupid enough to walk into the jungle unarmed should know he's bound to get hurt. So I planned to take his money and run.

I had two of my gang members, Tico and Hector, with me. They crouched on the ground behind me, waiting for the word to pounce. The man turned the corner and headed in our direction, and at just the right moment I screamed and jumped on him. We hit him and beat him, breaking his nose and dislocating his jaw. I can still hear him screaming, "Please don't hurt me," over and over. But his cries meant nothing. I had no sense of morals, no hint of conscience within me. He had money and I wanted it, and that was the only thing that mattered.

Tico and Hector held him down, but he wouldn't give us his wallet.

We kept hitting and hitting him, and he kept screaming for help, but he wouldn't cooperate. We told him to shut up, but he kept shouting, kept yelling, louder and louder. I knew I had to quiet him, so I took out my gun and held it to his head.

"Shut up," I screamed. "Shut up or I'll kill you." Over and over I cursed him and threatened him, yet he wouldn't stop yelling.

"Kill him, Nicky," my boys shouted. "Kill him before the cops hear."

I moved closer and put the barrel of my pistol to his forehead to get his attention, but he continued to scream. "I mean it," I cursed. "Shut up now or I'll kill you."

Still he shouted like a man possessed. So I pulled the trigger.

Click. No bullet. I lifted the gun to look at it, then again put it to his forehead. I pulled the trigger once more.

Click. Still no bullet. Over and over I pulled the trigger. *Click, click, click...* Six times I shot, and six times the gun misfired, though I knew it was loaded and in good working order. My boys grew angrier. The man looked up at me with terror in his eyes. He couldn't believe he was still alive.

I reached into his pocket and pulled out a large wallet, then hit him in the face with the butt of my gun. I jammed his wallet into my coat pocket and then beat him some more. We left him bloodied in the street.

Down the alley we ran, across the road and into another alley. We were certain we hadn't been seen, but suddenly, around the far corner, a police car screeched to a halt. Two blue uniforms jumped out and started running after us.

We instinctively split up and ran down different alleyways. I flew as fast as my feet would carry me, over a fence, around a corner, up a fire escape, across the top of a tall building, back down to the street. My coat kept slowing me down, so I stripped it off and slammed it into a trash can as I passed by. Now my feet were even faster, and I continued to run.

I left the policemen in the dust behind me. When I knew I had outrun them, I ran all the way to my apartment building, up the stairs, and into my dingy one-room flat.

I sat on the edge of the bed and caught my breath. Blood and sweat dripped off my fingers and onto the floor. The gun was gone...and so was the wallet! My coat...?

I suddenly remembered that I had stuck the gun and the wallet in my coat—the coat that I had thrown into the trash. I cursed again, then moved into the bathroom to wash up.

As I stood over the sink, scrubbing blood and dirt and sweat off my face and hands, out of my hair and fingernails, a cold chill swept over me. My spine shook with terror. *What have I done? What have I become? Is this who I am? A thief? A murderer? An animal in the streets?*

The horror of the event left me reeling in questions and confusion. I'd done so many horrible things in my life, things no man should ever do, yet for some reason this time it felt different. This time I nearly killed a man with my own hands. This time I had sunk to the depths of depravity. No...far lower. I had sunk to the very depths of hell.

Satan's Playground

To this day I don't understand what kept my gun from going off, but I know that God was the one who stopped it. He didn't have to protect me. I had done nothing to deserve such a gift. I could have easily killed the man and gone to prison for the rest of my life, as so many others in my situation have done. In fact, that's probably what I deserved. But God had other plans for me. He intervened for a reason, and I have spent my entire life in absolute gratitude for that moment.

That event happened just months before my conversion. Just months before I gave my heart to Jesus and my life to God forever. Just months before I finally found something worth living for.

There is a darkness so hollow and deep and hopeless that it slowly, agonizingly chokes the life out of all it envelops. It is a darkness that knows no meaning, a lifeless prison of despair. It grabs its victims and holds them by the throat, laughing, taunting, gradually sucking the life out of their veins.

And so many have found themselves trapped in its clutches. So many live each day in this dungeon of nothingness.

So often I'm asked why I think Satan has such a foothold on the inner city. In my gut I know the answer, yet I always struggle to explain it in words. Unless you've lived in hopelessness, you can never quite comprehend it.

There is a name for Satan's strength in the ghetto: it's called *poverty.*

Poverty can lead people to do desperate things—things they would otherwise never consider. It can create a sense of loneliness and despair like nothing else. A sense that no one cares, not even those closest to you; that life has abandoned you, passed you by, left you for dead in a cold, dank gutter; a sense that you are all alone in the world and completely invisible to those who pass by.

Before Jesus saved me from this dungeon of nothingness, I was living in a tiny, filthy one-room flat in the poorest section of Brooklyn. I had no skills, no hope of getting a decent job, no hope of a better education. I paid fifteen dollars a week for rent, and it was often all I could do to come up with the money. I had to steal, bribe, scheme every day just to put food in my belly. Having enough left over to pay for another week of shelter at times seemed impossible.

One time my friend Carlos, the president of our gang, asked me, "Nicky, how do you support yourself?" I avoided answering by making some stupid joke, because I was ashamed to tell him how much of a scavenger I was. Even Carlos had a means of getting money, but I was just an animal. The things I did privately, away from the gang, were even more dangerous than the things I did with them. In the gang we stole for drugs and liquor, but most of our time was spent protecting our turf. We were drunk with power and prejudice. But at the end of the day, I would find my way home, my stomach grumbling from hunger, my pockets completely empty.

Poverty creates an attitude within you like nothing else. It's a ghetto attitude, a mind-set that says, *It's not fair for you to have money when I'm broke and hungry. It's not fair for you to eat while I starve.* You begin to look at other people as simply a way to get what you need. If you are broke and they have money, you believe that you have the right to take it. And they have no right to keep it from you.

That is the lie Satan uses to keep his foothold on the inner city. He reaches into a dark and lonely heart and begins to twist and turn and manipulate until you lose all sight of reality. You lose sight of the truth. You lose all sense of right and wrong.

And if he can only keep you there, keep feeding you lies, keep blinding you to the truth, his foothold is secure.

Setting Captives Free

The war against evil should be seen, first and foremost, as a war on poverty. It should be a mission to completely stamp out the despair of hunger and fear and hopelessness that so permeates the poorest corners of the world.

To free every soul caught in the trap of loneliness and isolation. To take away the poverty that gives Satan such strength and power and effectiveness within the ghettos of our culture. "Is not this the kind of fasting I have chosen," said God through his prophet Isaiah, "to loose the chains of injustice and untie the cords of the yoke, to set the oppressed free and break every yoke? Is it not to share your food with the hungry and to provide the poor wanderer with shelter—when you see the naked, to clothe him, and not to turn away from your own flesh and blood?" (Isaiah 58:6-7).

How can we continue to sit back in apathy when poverty runs so rampant and when God is so clear about what he expects us to do about it? What is it going to take for the church to finally rise up and say in one voice, "We will no longer allow this to go on!" How long before we open our eyes to the masses among us still caught in the chains of bondage—the masses enslaved by Satan and blinded by the plight of poverty?

That we have allowed it to go on this long is the greatest of all human tragedies.

So many Christians have never experienced life in this dungeon of nothingness. They have no concept of how dark and lonely it can be, no idea how desperate you can become in the claws of hopelessness. They look at the inner city and wonder why people do the things they do, why they stay there, how they can be so stupid. They see something they don't understand.

When I look at the inner city, I see myself. I see where I might still be had I never been saved by Jesus, had I never found a hope greater than my desperation, had I never had my eyes opened to the lies of Satan. I see the darkness that once held me captive, and all I can think about is making my way back down to light a candle and show others the way out.

If you've never felt the joy and satisfaction of setting a captive free from slavery, of reaching into the darkness and lighting a candle of truth, of holding a blind soul in your arms as he takes his first glimpse of light, I beg you to begin working toward it today. Begin looking for ways to loose the chains of poverty and injustice. Begin unbuckling the yoke, just within your sphere of influence. Begin sharing your food with the hungry, providing shelter to the wanderers, giving clothes to the poor and naked.

And while you're at it, tell them about Jesus. Tell them about the Cross and the forgiveness that Jesus brings. Help open their eyes to the truth.

Show them that there is life outside the dungeon of nothingness.

CHAPTER FIVE

THE COWARDICE OF SATAN

There is a truth about America that I hesitate to mention. I risk offending a lot of my good friends by saying it. But when we think of poverty in America, what usually comes to mind is people of color, mostly African Americans and Latinos. We think of our country as a white world, and we discount those who are not.

We call the ghetto "trash" and at the same time identify it with minorities. What does that say to people of color? What does it say to those who are forced to live in the inner city about how they are seen by the rest of the world? How does it make them feel?

One of the things that struck me during our outreach in Oslo was how few minorities we saw, yet hopelessness reigned throughout the country. Drugs are so prominent that scores of people walked around in a daze, confused and helpless. I saw beautiful people with blond hair, blue eyes, and fine clothes completely bound by Satan. Drugs had so ravaged their minds and bodies that they seemed almost lifeless. Like the joy had been completely sucked from their lives. It reminded me again that ghettos come in all forms and shapes. This war against Satan is not a battle of colors; it's a battle for souls.

It's true that the inner cities of America are desperate and violent places and that many who live there are minorities. Blood runs through the streets of the ghetto like water. But that blood is as red as yours and mine. When an African American man bleeds, his blood runs red, not black. When a Latino is cut, he bleeds red, not brown. When an Anglo bleeds, he bleeds red, not white. Inside we are all the same. We are flesh and bones and blood and heart! We are brothers and sisters of humanity, all the same in the eyes of God.

And until we see that truth, put aside our feelings of prejudice and inequality, we will never be able to effectively combat the lies of Satan. The lies that say to others, "You're trash because you're poor." The only trash is evil, and that's where the battle should be fought.

AT WAR IN THE BRONX

Even now my mind is fresh with the faces of helplessness I saw in the heart of the Bronx this past summer. Faces of all shapes and colors and ages. Beautiful boys and girls, men and women, blacks, whites, Spanish, Asians. So many were lost. So many needed Jesus.

We were in the final stages of our six-week TRUCE outreach to the inner cities of New York. For weeks we had been evangelizing in the streets, conducting Hit 'n' Run events on neighborhood corners throughout the city, all the while inviting people to our final outreach in the Bronx. At every Hit 'n' Run, more souls were saved, but there was still so much to be done.

I remember standing on the platform in front of several thousand people packed along the street in front of me. Our stage was set up at the end of a long, narrow street in the heart of one of the most drug-infested neighborhoods in all of New York. High-rise apartment buildings towered overhead on either side. Policemen surrounded the perimeter, watching carefully for any sign of trouble.

For several seconds I just stood, surveying the crowd before me. Gang colors were everywhere. Prostitutes and pushers and addicts were scattered throughout the crowd, waiting to hear what I had to say. I glanced at the buildings surrounding us and noticed people hanging out of their windows, children crowded on fire escapes, teens huddled together on rickety balconies and metal stairways. Mothers and fathers watching through open screens. So many eyes, all looking to me. Waiting. Watching. Wondering.

I felt so small and helpless standing in front of them. Once again I knew that nothing I had to say could make a difference. Nothing I could do would erase the pain. It was all up to Jesus. What these people needed was a miracle, and only God could provide that. Only God could bring hope to this hopeless corner of the world.

Dear Jesus, I prayed in my heart. *Look at them. So many souls. So many poor and hurting people—people who need you. People who are trapped in a sea of poverty and danger and evil. Open their eyes, Lord. Touch their hearts. Use my words to bring them to you!*

As I stood before the crowd, I knew in my heart that Jesus could heal them, that he *would* heal them, if only they would open up and let him come in. If only they could see past their desperation and into God's merciful heart.

Sending Satan Back to Hell

As I began to speak, to share my testimony, I sensed a calmness falling on the neighborhood. I couldn't get over how attentive people became. They hung on every word. And I knew it wasn't me—they were mesmerized by the power of the Holy Spirit. I could feel their sense of wonder and expectation. Just moments earlier I had felt the presence of evil, the hardness of the Bronx, the stronghold of Satan, but now it was beginning to lift. It's something I've felt thousands of times in thousands of different neighborhoods, yet it never ceases to amaze me. The feeling is impossible to describe yet very real. It is the presence of God. It is the wholesale retreat of the Enemy as God's Spirit moves in and settles on a crowd of people. It is the Holy Spirit working, convicting, literally beating the hell out of people's hearts and lives!

And it is a precious, magnificent feeling. A sacred thing to experience.

The feeling came over me with such force that I could hardly contain my emotions. I don't always do this, but I felt God telling me to acknowledge this feeling to the audience. "Just a few hours ago, Satan owned this neighborhood," I shouted. "Those of you who live here know what I mean. He rules this place. You can feel him, sense him, taste his evil. But at this moment, he's no longer here. Jesus is here! God is in control!"

No one moved or looked away as I spoke. They knew exactly what I meant—you could see it in their expressions, in their faces, through the pleading of their eyes. They knew something was different.

"What you feel now is the presence of God. At this moment Satan can't touch you—he has no hold on this street. He is like a frightened child cowering in fear right now. You don't have to be afraid of him. You don't have anything to fear. Jesus is here, and he loves you. God is drawing you to himself. I know you can feel it. I know you can sense him calling you."

As I spoke I could feel the Holy Spirit enveloping the crowd, working on their hearts, bringing so many to conviction. Throughout the crowd people were crying and breaking down in remorse. I knew at that moment that if I didn't say another word, God would still have the victory. He was in control. He was moving powerfully among us.

My emotion got the best of me, and I raised an angry fist toward the sky and shouted, "Do you hear that, Devil? Do you hear what I'm saying? You have no power here! You are nothing! You are no longer welcome here! Go to hell where you belong, because tonight Jesus is in charge!"

Before I had a chance to invite people forward to accept Jesus, dozens streamed toward the stage, falling on their knees to the ground in repentance. I motioned for the workers to come forward and pray with them as I continued speaking. I looked at the buildings around us and noticed kids and parents crying in their windows. One young woman in the building to my left reached her arms out toward me, as if pleading for salvation. Several workers quickly made their way into her building and to her apartment to pray with her. I reached my hand out in her direction and invited her to accept Jesus into her heart. Tears streamed down her face as the Holy Spirit called her to Christ. She dug her face into her mother's arms and wept.

Hundreds came forward to receive Jesus that night. God brought such a wave of conviction that we were overwhelmed by the response. We stayed late into the night, praying for them, helping them receive Christ, and doing our best to get everyone's name on response cards for follow-up in the future.

Women who were walking these streets just hours earlier to sell their bodies were now on their knees before God, pleading for forgiveness. Men who had come to this street corner tonight looking for drugs or sex or both were now standing before Jesus in repentance. We were completely in awe of the work that God was doing in this hurting, forsaken neighborhood.

PROTECT THE PROTECTORS

I came down from the stage to help pray with the people who had come forward, and Sal, one of our lead singers, took my place on stage. At the microphone he again encouraged people to give their hearts to Jesus. "Don't leave tonight without discovering the power of Jesus," he said. "Let God change your heart and life forever."

As he was speaking, several of the policemen assigned to the area came to the base of the stage to get his attention. One was wearing a white shirt and black tie—obviously a detective or police lieutenant. They all had tears in their eyes, and the man in the suit said to Sal, "Could you please pray for us? Pray for all the New York policemen and the policemen in the Bronx. Please pray for our safety."

Sal was visibly moved by his request, and he immediately asked the crowd to quiet down while he prayed for the law officers. "Dear Jesus, you know how much these policemen and policewomen do to protect these cities from harm. And you know the danger that they put themselves in. Lord, they need your help. They need your guidance. They need your Holy Spirit to go before them as they keep peace in the city.

"Lord, right now, please bring a special anointing on the men and women surrounding us—all the police within the Bronx and all of New York. Shield them, protect them, send your angels to surround them. Keep them from harm as they work so hard each day to keep the cities safe."

The crowd was so moved by Sal's sincere prayer that they broke out in cheers and applause, facing the policemen behind the stage. It was just one example of the love and respect that comes upon people when the Spirit of the Lord moves in their midst.

Time to Rise Up

No matter how many times I experience the power of God, I never get used to it. I never grow complacent with the way he can bring even the coldest, hardest neighborhood to conviction. The way he can dissipate evil within a matter of seconds and expose the deepest parts of a person's heart, bringing him to his knees before the cross.

No matter how much it seems that Satan is winning this war, I know that it's just a matter of time before God steps in and takes charge, before God blows his breath, sending the devil cowering into a dark corner.

Standing on that platform in the Bronx, feeling the power of God's Spirit settling on us, moving among us, blowing like a cool northern wind, I felt completely invigorated. Like I could defeat Satan with just one blow to his temple. Like I could take on all the forces of evil and send them back to hell! It's something I feel every time the anointing of God is near. Every time his Spirit takes charge. Every time we go to battle against evil with Jesus by our side.

You could feel God moving among the crowd, ministering, healing, doing miracles in the hearts of those who needed him. His Spirit echoed between the buildings, moving in and out of windows and doors, between corridors, down hallways, into apartments. Hearts of sin were broken. Minds of filth were filled with thoughts of remorse and shame. Bodies ravaged with drugs felt the healing power of salvation.

This is how God works. This is how he moves. This is where you'll find him at war with Satan. And in the middle of this war is where I most long to be.

Too often I hear Christians fretting and complaining about the future.

They cry and moan about Satan's many victories in the world, how he is winning so many battles and gaining so much momentum in this country, as well as around the world. They talk as if Satan is destined to win. "We're losing our kids to the culture," they say. "Our churches are dying in numbers, and our society is growing more evil by the day."

I'm not blind to what's going on. I see it myself, and it makes me just as angry. But I also know that when you see Satan winning, it's because the people of God are cowering in retreat. They are giving up too easily. They are busy licking their wounds from injuries in battle instead of standing up and facing the Enemy with even greater courage.

If there is one thing we have learned through our ministry—through facing the Enemy on his own turf time and time again, day after day, week after week—it is that Satan is a coward. He is a sniveling worm who picks on the most defenseless among us, the most hopeless and desperate. Like a playground bully who runs for cover as soon as a kid his size shows up, Satan retreats at the first sign of real power.

If we don't see him running with his tail between his bony legs, it is only because we haven't stood up to him with any true authority. We haven't given him reason enough to fear us.

Do we truly understand the power we have at our fingertips? Do we grasp the significance of the message that we bring to a lost world? Do we comprehend how easily evil can be beaten and revoked by simply opening ourselves up to the moving of the Holy Spirit among us?

Do we know what God is capable of doing among us?

How I long to see a day when Christians stand shoulder to shoulder, arm in arm, in this war with Satan and finally draw a line in the sand, right in the middle of his path. A line that stops him dead in his tracks. A line that says, "You've had your day! You've had your fun! But your day is over. In the name of Jesus, you can go no further!"

I long to see an army of soldiers rise up against him. A regiment of soul-obsessed believers, taking up arms in this fight against evil. An army of men and women with hearts that burn for God and lives dedicated to his will.

Isn't that the kind of army you long to be a part of? Don't you wish you could play even a small part in such a huge battle for God? Isn't this what you've been waiting for, what you've been hoping for, what you've been praying and believing that God would bring your way?

If so, then God wants you to know that the army is already in place. The war is already being waged. All you have to do is take up your sword and find your place within his ranks!

CHAPTER SIX

IN THE SPIRIT'S WAKE

How many of us truly understand what it means to walk in the Spirit of God, to live with the passion of Jesus, to trust in God with a faith that is raw and genuine and powerful? A faith that knows no limits and fears nothing? A faith that can stare the devil in the eyes and say, "You can go no farther! You have no more control over me! You are weak and exposed and impotent!"

A faith that can move any mountain, no matter how high or wide or difficult.

Yet that's the kind of faith that God demands of those who want to see his power. It's the only thing that can activate the true might and authority of the Holy Spirit in our lives.

I could fill a book with stories of people who live that kind of life. People who move in the Spirit so eloquently and powerfully that they literally change the world around them. People whose hearts burn with a soul obsession and, because of it, who have made a greater impact on the kingdom than most of us would ever dare to dream.

POWER IN PUERTO RICO

One of those people is Pastor Marilu Dones, a dear and precious friend who, along with her husband, Pastor Carlos Dones Reyes, ministers through one of the largest churches in Puerto Rico—more than three thousand members strong. Together they have built one of the most powerful, passionate ministries in all of Puerto Rico, maybe even the world. They are loved and respected throughout Puerto Rico for the work they do. The governor loves them, and their church is as diverse as any church I've known—doctors, lawyers, judges, and politicians worshiping alongside the poor and middle class.

Marilu is a humble, godly woman, bright and sophisticated, yet very down to earth. And Carlos is one of the kindest, most faithful servants I've ever known. People flock to their church from miles around just to hear them speak.

As a female pastor, Marilu has come under a lot of criticism from other churches, but all you have to do is look at the fruits of her ministry to know that God has placed a special anointing on her. The people of Puerto Rico have nothing but respect and admiration for her, even those who don't attend her church.

She has a weekly television program that's viewed throughout the island, and she never asks for money. So many people expect her to try to use the forum to raise funds for her ministry, like so many other television evangelists, yet it never comes. Many preachers wonder how she stays on the air without pleading for support, but she knows that God is the only support she needs.

One Sunday morning several years ago, in the middle of her church's worship service, the Holy Spirit instructed her to stop the service and send her people out on a prayer walk. She got up in the pulpit and told her congregation, "We're not going to have a sermon today. Instead we're going to live one. I want everyone to follow me into the streets. We're going to walk and pray and evangelize wherever the Spirit takes us. Grab your Bibles and purses and follow me."

I don't think she even took time for the collection that morning. Marilu has never worried about money. She always knew that God would make up any shortfall in their budget. Her job was to follow the leading of the Spirit, and that's all she was interested in.

The congregation followed Carlos and Marilu out the front door, down the steps, and into the heart of the city. The young people of the church heard what was going on and left their classes to follow her. Down the streets and along the highway they walked and prayed and sang together. She felt the Spirit telling her to start evangelizing the neighborhood, so that's what she instructed her people to do. The congregation split up into groups and took off in different directions, going door to door, ministering as the Holy Spirit led them.

At each house they went to, people were surprised to see a group of Christians outside of church on a Sunday morning. People were thrilled to talk and pray with them. That morning Carlos and Marilu put feet to the church, literally taking church to the streets, the way Jesus would have done.

At one point Marilu's group passed by a business that was well known throughout the community as a place to buy drugs. The owner's car was outside, so Marilu went to talk with him. She knocked on the door several times before getting his attention, and he wasn't happy to see them. "We want to pray for you and your business," she told him. But he resisted.

"I don't need your prayers," he said. "Leave me alone."

Again she insisted that he let her pray for him, but he wouldn't listen. He mocked her and told her to leave. She persisted in her effort to reach him, explaining that God had put a strong sense on her heart to pray for him, that she feared something bad would happen to him. She prophesied over the man, giving him a strong warning. "If you don't let me pray for you, I'm afraid that harm will come to your business," she told him. But still he refused. He told her to leave and slammed the door in her face.

Standing across the street from the man's building, Marilu told her congregation, "He can stop us from praying for him inside, but nothing is stopping us from praying for him on the street." So she began praying for the man's soul. She prayed that the Lord would bring him under conviction and that his soul would be saved. She prayed that God would bind Satan from infecting any more people through the man's drug dealing. In a stroke of boldness, she prayed, "Lord, you know the harm that this man brings to our city, and we will no longer tolerate it. In the name of Jesus, we bind Satan here and now. We demand that Satan have no more power over this neighborhood, no more hold on this business, and no more influence within this community. We will no longer tolerate evil in this community!"

Exactly three days later, during a New Year celebration, Marilu was informed that the owner of the business had been found dead by the police. Some thieves had broken into his business to rob him, and when he tried to stop them, they beheaded him, leaving him in a pool of blood on the floor.

The business never opened again. It remains stained by the owner's blood. The news of this man's demise saddened the congregation, especially Marilu. The Lord tried to warn him, but he wouldn't listen.

Help After a Hurricane

In 1998 Hurricane George pounded the island of Puerto Rico, causing enormous damage to property and taking many lives in the process. It was one of the worst hurricanes in the island's history, wreaking havoc on towns throughout the region, including the communities surrounding the Doneses' church.

As soon as the hurricane wound down, Carlos and Marilu mobilized the church to help. They responded the way Jesus would respond—by providing food and shelter and clothing to anyone who had need. They dug out the church's gas generator and set up a makeshift kitchen. People from the surrounding communities flocked to the building for food and water, and no one was turned away. They never worried about the cost, just provided what was needed to everyone who came. They fed people three meals a day and used the church as a base of operation, working alongside the Red Cross and Department of Social Services to provide shelter and food and medicine.

Two days into their relief effort, some thieves stole their generator, but the church was unfazed. Marilu told them to build a fire instead, and that's how they cooked the hundreds of meals they were providing each day. When people couldn't travel to the church to eat, she would send food to them wherever they were.

Many families deep in the woods and mountains were without food and water, and no one was able to reach them by car. The roads were covered with fallen trees and rocks and mud. So each day Marilu packed a large bag and carried it on foot through the forests, up the hills, far into the forests, to the doorsteps of those who had no other means of help. She trekked for miles through rocks and vines to reach them. Her legs were bruised and scratched from the trip. Many men were afraid to make the long and treacherous journey, so she did it herself. And she never complained. She knew that if she didn't help them, they would have to go without, so she did what Jesus would have done.

For six months the church worked to restore their community. Through the entire ordeal they never stopped helping, in spite of the strain it put on their budget and the time it took from their ministry. One by one the people started getting back on their feet. Life on the island was finally getting back to normal, and people no longer needed their help.

But through the process, the church discovered a lot of elderly people in the community who needed continued help, so to this day the church still feeds them and cares for them on a daily basis, bringing hot meals to their doorsteps each morning.

No church in all of Puerto Rico has had the kind of impact that this church has made on their community. No two pastors have done more to increase the kingdom and save people from hell than Pastors Marilu and Carlos Dones Reyes. They are true testaments to what can be accomplished on earth by the power of the Holy Spirit working through the lives of two humble, soul-obsessed servants of God.

A CHILDLIKE FAITH

It's impossible for me to talk about passion without thinking of Steve Pineda. Steve was a former drug addict who came to Christ through the ministry of Victory Outreach—which was founded by my good friend and spiritual son, Sonny Arguinzoni.

Steve grew up on the streets and had been to prison several times. But then he came to Christ and his life changed completely. He developed a passion for Jesus and became the pastor of a Victory Outreach church in Hayward, California. Steve was always talking about Jesus, always reaching out, always on fire for the Lord, and nothing could quench his spirit.

One day Steve felt a burden in his spirit to evangelize in the Philippines. He didn't have any money or support, but he was sure God wanted him to go. Friends told him he was nuts. But one day he packed a suitcase, scraped together enough money for a ticket, and boarded a plane. He arrived in Manila with nothing but a suitcase of clothes and a few dollars in his pocket—not even enough to buy a room for the night.

You can imagine the scene. Here he was, a missionary with no support and no funds, walking through the streets of the city, not knowing a soul, wondering where his next meal would come from. But that was Steve. He had the faith of a child—completely innocent and irrational.

For several days Steve walked the streets of Manila, praying and seeking God. He knew that God had a mission for him; he just didn't know what it was. He met with several pastors in the area before finding one who took him under his wings.

For a week Steve stayed in Manila, talking with people, getting to know the community, praying for God's vision. And soon God made it clear that he was to found a school of evangelism in the Philippines. He had no idea how to do such a thing and no experience with fund-raising, but he believed God and began sharing this vision. A week later he was back in California, where he set to work to carry this dream to fruition.

Because of Steve's impact on the community in Manila, he was able to convince people to give money to the project. The governor encouraged him and did all he could to help. Soon the center was built, and still today evangelists are being trained in Manila each year through this vision that God laid on Steve's heart.

He later built another center for evangelism in Hayward, California, again with no money of his own, only a vision from God.

That's typical of how Steve lived his life. Nothing he did seemed very sane from a human standpoint; he just trusted God and moved where he felt God leading.

One day I was speaking at a crusade, and Steve came up afterward to talk to me. He said he was moved by my testimony and wanted to pledge a large amount of money to our ministry. I laughed aloud and said to him, "That's very generous, Steve, but you don't have any money! Thanks for the offer, but I won't hold you to it."

He argued with me and told me that he knew God would help him complete his pledge. "God will give me the money," he said. "Don't worry."

We joked and laughed together for several minutes, and before our conversation had ended a woman came over to talk to Steve. She was an old friend of his, and she looked very serious. "God put it on my heart to give you this money," she said, handing Steve a check. "I'm not sure why, but I know God wants you to have it."

Steve accepted the check graciously, thanked the woman for her generosity, then turned and handed the check to me.

I learned more about raw faith from Steve than any man I've ever met. We became good friends through the years, and his trust in God never wavered.

Faith to the End

Some years later Steve developed hepatitis C and eventually ended up in the hospital dying of cancer. His years as a drug addict had finally caught up with him. I remember talking with Steve one day, about a month before his death, as he shared his heart with me. He admitted that he had known for eight or nine years that he was in danger, that the doctors had repeatedly warned him to get into some kind of treatment, but he had ignored their warnings. He wanted to believe that God would heal him of the disease, and he set the matter to prayer. "I could have beaten this if I had just listened to the doctors," he told me. He now understood that God had been trying to warn him. His sweet wife, Josie, now had on her shoulders the responsibility of raising their children on her own.

That's the kind of guy Steve was. When he should have been worrying about his health, he was so busy trying to evangelize and bring others to the Lord that he forgot about himself. Josie was concerned for him and tried to get him to see the doctor, but he kept putting it off, kept trying to do more for the Lord, kept thinking of the needs of others instead of his own. Eventually it caught up with him.

Steve cried over the thought of leaving his wife and children alone. He knew he had made a mistake. He stayed home with his family as long as he could, but soon the disease had completely overtaken him. It was clear that he didn't have long to live, so Josie admitted him to the hospital.

Even days away from death, with his strength completely gone and cancer ravaging his body, Steve continued to preach about Jesus. He lay in the hospital bed witnessing to every person who came into his room, from the nurses and doctors to the people cleaning the floors and changing his sheets.

One day Steve had been spitting up blood, and a custodian came to the room to change his sheets. Steve was holding a towel over his mouth and apologizing for the mess, but he couldn't help but witness about Jesus. He could hardly talk and couldn't even hold his head up straight, yet here he was preaching about the goodness of God. His wife and children sat on the other side of him, but he turned his attention away from them in order to try and lead this man to the Lord.

The man was so moved that he cried. He couldn't believe what he was seeing. Here was Steve dying of cancer, yet his heart was filled with nothing but faith and hope. The custodian broke down and asked Steve to pray with him. Right there in the hospital room, Steve led the man to Jesus.

Another time Steve was sitting with his family in the hospital lobby when he noticed another man he recognized—someone he knew to be a backslider. The man had turned his back on God and the church. Right there in the lobby, Steve confronted him about it. "You need to come back to Jesus," he told the young man. "Find a church and give your life back to God!" Before long the man was overtaken by guilt, and he prayed with Steve, promising to find a church and remain faithful.

Even through unimaginable pain, Steve was more focused on leading people to Christ than he was on his own condition.

Steve grew worse as the days went by, and soon he was at death's door. His pain was unbearable, so the nurses treated him with morphine. Sonny Arguinzoni flew in numerous times to see him during his last few weeks, and it broke his heart to see Steve dying. Many other pastors and friends came to visit him, but Steve insisted to Josie that he didn't want them to see him. He was embarrassed by the way he looked, so thin and frail. He told his wife, "Don't let them see me like this. Tell them I love them, but I can't talk right now."

Josie understood his concern, but she knew that people wanted to see him one last time. So she brought his friends in one at a time. Steve was so overtaken by pain and drugs that he didn't even realize what was going on.

Just before he passed away, Josie brought their children to sit by his side. They sat stroking his head and holding his hand. They prayed with him and sang to him, talking him into eternity. His young son, Estevan, held his hand until his very last breath. The boy talked to his father, telling him what a beautiful father he had been and how much they all loved him. He talked to him about heaven and the reward awaiting him there. He talked about Jesus.

As the boy was speaking, his mother reached over and took his hand. "Your father has gone to be with the Lord," she said. The boy started to cry, and she held his hand tighter. "Don't be sad," she said. "He took us with him in his heart. Your father was a great man of God."

SISTER ELSIE

Sister Elsie Minor is another example of someone who lives and moves in the blessing of God. Today, at more than eighty years of age, she is a living legend in Harlem. Elsie came to the Lord at the age of forty after a long, hard life on the streets. She had spent most of her life in bars, drinking and doing drugs, sleeping with any man who came along. She lived an extremely sinful life, and her testimony usually shocks people who hear it for the first time.

Elsie came to Jesus through the work of the Soul Saving Station, a dynamic church in Harlem. And she has never looked back.

The young people of her church today can't imagine her previous life of sin. Elsie is so sweet and tender and loving. She takes young people under her wings and mentors them, prays for them, prays with them, imparts her anointing on their lives. She is a precious woman of the Lord with a powerful faith.

Elsie takes the bus wherever she goes, and the bus drivers often won't let her pay for her rides. She's done so much for her community that they're just happy to have her on board. Everyone knows and respects her. And she witnesses for the Lord at every opportunity.

She often says to the young people she mentors, "The old know the way, but the young have the strength to do the running." Sister Elsie has gained her godly wisdom through years of study and prayer and experience, and she imparts that wisdom to the youth in her church. Every week she sits at the back of the auditorium, praying for the young, and they flock to her side just to be around her. She's done more harm to the devil through praying and mentoring than most people could ever hope to accomplish.

The body of Christ needs more people like Sister Elsie Minor. People who love the Lord with a passion and exude his love for others. People who are a daily blessing to others, because they move in the blessing of God!

Educated by the Holy Spirit

There is nothing as exhilarating as walking each day with the Holy Spirit. Moving and breathing in the power of God. Listening for the voice that comes to your spirit, then obeying, whatever he would have you do. Going wherever he tells you to go. Saying what he tells you to say. Ministering to whomever he puts in your path. Drinking from the well of his wisdom as he imparts it into your heart and mind.

I love living in the wake of the Holy Spirit! There's nothing I'd rather be doing than following him into battle. I try to never question his ways, never doubt his insight, never hesitate to let him lead.

So many people try to educate the Holy Spirit on what he should do. I've heard preachers talk about how the Holy Spirit works, what the Holy Spirit thinks, and what he does and doesn't want us to do. I wonder if they've ever stopped to ask the Holy Spirit's permission to talk for him!

God's Spirit doesn't answer to you and me. He doesn't ask us what we think about his ways. He only asks us to follow. You can't outsmart him, and you can seldom figure him out. He's like a package of surprises, waiting each day to open up for us new doors of ministry and excitement and experiences. The minute you think you understand him, he surprises you once again.

The Holy Spirit's greatest enemy is our day planner! He's not interested in working his way into our schedule; he wants to *become* our schedule. To guide us through our day, not help us plan it. To shake us from our daily routines and rituals and get us to turn loose and trust him.

The most powerful and effective prayer any of us can pray is to say, "Jesus, I release my life to the working of your Holy Spirit. I have no plans of my own, no agenda, no goals of my own choosing, no desire that isn't placed in my spirit by yours. I turn loose of my life and schedule. I renounce Satan's hold on my life and the sins that enslave me. Take me Lord! Show me where you want me to go, what you want me to do, who you want me to see, and what you want me to say. I am no longer going to limit your work in my life. Take me! Mold me! Use me! Lead me! Make me a vessel of your Spirit!"

Instead of spending your life praying for blessings, pray that God will use you to bless others. Instead of striving to be comfortable and wealthy and well-fed, pray that God will use you to help others find comfort and shelter and food. Instead of looking for miracles, let God turn your life into a living, breathing miracle of his will.

That's how you make a true impact on the world for Christ. That's how you create the kind of influence that Pastors Marilu Dones and Carlos Dones Reyes have created within their community. That's how you change your world the way that Sister Elsie Minor has done. The way you leave a legacy like the one left by Steve Pineda.

If you want to change the world, begin by letting God change you. By letting the passion of Jesus become your passion. By letting the Holy Spirit be your only guide and mentor every step, every minute of the day. By allowing God to set your heart on fire with a soul obsession!

And the LORD said, "I will cause all my goodness
to pass in front of you, and I will proclaim my
name, the LORD, in your presence. I will have
mercy on whom I will have mercy, and I will have
compassion on whom I will have compassion."

EXODUS 33:19

Remember not the sins of my youth and my
rebellious ways; according to your love remember me,
for you are good, O LORD.

PSALM 25:7

I love the LORD, for he heard my voice;
he heard my cry for mercy.

PSALM 116:1

Go home to your family and tell them
how much the Lord has done for you,
and how he has had mercy on you.

MARK 5:19

Therefore, as God's chosen people, holy and dearly
loved, clothe yourselves with compassion, kindness,
humility, gentleness and patience.

COLOSSIANS 3:12

Be merciful to those who doubt; snatch others from
the fire and save them; to others show mercy.

JUDE 22-23

CHAPTER SEVEN

A KISS FROM HEAVEN

I haven't run across many kids who frightened me in the last forty years, but Alberto came close. I understand more than most that hardened teens who look tough are often insecure and afraid. They hide their fear behind a facade of tattoos, gang colors, and gaudy jewelry, but I'm not fooled. I see through their pretense and into their souls, into their hearts.

But Alberto was a different story. His eyes were so cold and lifeless that even I couldn't see through them. When I looked at him the first time, I saw nothing—no fear, pain, or remorse. But God showed me otherwise.

It was several years ago, and I was speaking at two different high schools in Houston, Texas. The schools were in the most poverty-stricken areas of town, and gangs had been wreaking havoc on the grounds for years. The teachers and principals were threatened on a regular basis, and many were afraid to come to work each morning. I was asked to speak to the kids about the problem of gangs and violence.

Often when I address kids at their schools, I face a wall of indifference from the start. They don't want to hear what I have to say. Most try to keep up a good front for their friends, but in my heart I know they are listening. I know I am getting through—at least to some. So I persist.

I hold nothing back when I talk in high schools. Principals know before I come that I'm going to do more than talk about the dangers of violence and drugs and sex and gangs; I'm going to talk about Jesus. My testimony is for God's glory, and that's the only way I'm willing to use it. If teachers are offended by religion, they'd better be prepared, because I pull no punches. What I know that many don't want to hear is that without Jesus there is no real solution to the problems plaguing society. He's the answer to every question, every problem they have. He's the only one who can truly turn kids away from their anger and hopelessness.

As usual, by the time I finished my talk in Houston, the room had grown still and silent. Kids who had come in laughing and joking were deathly quiet after hearing my testimony. They saw that I understood what they were going through, that I had been where they were, and that I saw through their tough and angry masks. And when I told them what Jesus had done for me, how he had pulled me from a life of despair, it made them think.

At the end of my testimony, I told them that I would be speaking at a nearby church and invited them to join me. When I do this, the teachers are usually surprised by how many of them show up. And it's often the most unlikely ones in the room—the biggest troublemakers in the school.

Alberto

Alberto was one of those kids. He was a gang leader and one of the most feared teens in Houston's inner city. The kid you would least expect to see in a church service. But he came.

More than fifteen hundred people showed up at the church that evening, completely filling the sanctuary. I spoke for three nights in a row, and we packed the building each time. Even the pastor was surprised at how many kids flocked to his building—kids who would never show up for a Sunday morning service or any other religious event. It's a true testament to how much these young people long to believe that there is something more to life than gangs and violence and drugs.

Alberto came with his mother that evening and sat near the back of the auditorium. The two sat silently as I gave my testimony.

Fifteen minutes into the service, Alberto suddenly became ill. He jumped up and ran out of the auditorium, to the nearest rest room, where he violently threw up. Several men standing nearby offered to help, but he refused. He washed his face and came back into the assembly. Ten minutes later he again ran out of the auditorium and into the rest room. Once more he threw up. The same men saw him and begged him to let them call a doctor, but still he refused. "I'm not leaving! I want to hear what this man has to say," he screamed at them before coming back into the auditorium.

Several more times Alberto was forced by sickness to leave the auditorium, but always he returned within a few minutes. He stayed through my entire testimony, sweating and shaking the entire time.

More than three hundred kids came forward that evening, many accepting Jesus for the first time. They were beautiful kids, lost kids, lonely kids—all longing for hope. I spent much time praying with them, and almost all of them waited patiently for me. So many kids accepted Jesus that night that I was floating on air with excitement.

At eleven in the evening, many kids were still waiting for prayer, and there were only a handful of us there to pray with them. We planned to stay all night if we had to. I looked up and saw pastor Eric Dicesare standing next to me.

"Nicky," he said, "there's a boy in my office who says he needs to talk to you. He wouldn't come forward. He's been waiting in the back for hours. I convinced him to wait for you in my office, but my staff is frightened of him."

"Who is he?" I asked.

"His name is Alberto. He's a gang leader in this area. He runs the whole school—the whole neighborhood. Everyone is afraid of him—the teachers, the principal, the parents. He's a dangerous boy, and no one knows why he came or what he wants with you, but no one in the church wants to go near him. He won't talk to anyone but you."

On the way to the pastor's office, he told me that the boy's mother was waiting for him in another room. He said that her eyes were black and swollen from a recent beating—no doubt at the hands of her son.

Alberto was staring straight ahead as I walked into the pastor's office. I moved over in front of him and stood, looking him straight in the eye. He said nothing, just looked at me. His shirt was sleeveless, and I caught a glimpse of his bulging biceps. On his right arm were five tattoos—all faces.

"Tell me about your tattoos," I asked him.

He glanced down at his arm, then back at me. "Those are my boys from my hood. They're all dead now."

I looked closer at his arm and noticed that one of the faces was different. It was bright red and evil looking, with horns coming out of the crown. The face of Satan.

"What about that one," I asked. "Is that the devil?"

"Yeah," he said, smirking and nodding his head. "Evil is what it's all about."

For the longest time the two of us stood face to face with each other as

I contemplated what to say to him. He never told me why he wanted to talk to me, and I never asked. I just waited and prayed. In my spirit I sensed God telling me, *Give him a hug.* The idea wasn't so appealing to me. The thought was more frightening than anything. He showed absolutely no emotion, no sense of remorse or fear. His eyes were cold and lifeless and angry.

I knew he wasn't there by accident. The Holy Spirit must have been working in his heart or he never would have come, never would have stayed, never would have asked to talk to me. *Inside he's just a scared little boy,* I thought. *Why else would he be here?*

So I did what God told me to do. I put my arms around him and drew his head to my chest. At first he resisted. His body grew tense and tight, yet he didn't fight me. He didn't pull away. I held him for a moment, still feeling the tension in his bones, before whispering into his ear, "You're hurting, aren't you, Son?"

I felt his body shake as I spoke. He started to pull away, but I held him tightly and whispered again, softly, so that no one else could hear. "I know you're hurting. I understand. Down deep you just want to be loved. Your father doesn't love you, and your mother doesn't know how. Life hasn't been fair to you—I know that. And God knows that. You've tried to hide your pain with evil. You've done things you're not proud of. But Jesus doesn't care—he loves you just as you are. Let Jesus love you."

In that instant I felt him melt into my arms. His body went limp and he began to cry. I wasn't expecting it. I didn't know I would get through to him so quickly. He sunk his head into my chest and sobbed like a baby. Several times I thought he was choking, he sobbed so loudly. I just held him and let him cry.

"Let me embrace your pain," I told him. "You've been fighting the world for so long, but all you're fighting is yourself. You're fighting God. You feel trapped. But Jesus can set you free. Don't fight him anymore."

For twenty minutes I held him as he wept in my arms. He threw his large arms around my back and held on tightly, clinging desperately, longingly. His head remained buried in my chest the entire time.

I prayed for him, and then I prayed with him as he repeated my words. He wanted to confess the evil he had done, so I let him. I listened as he told me of the people he had hurt, the sins he was so ashamed of. He told me of the times he had beaten his mother.

"I want you to do something for me," I said. "I want you to go and get your mother. Bring her in here. You need to tell her you're sorry for what you've done. You need to ask her forgiveness and to promise that you will never again lay a hand on her. Show Jesus how sorry you are."

Without hesitation he ran out of the room and returned with his mother by his side. She looked worried, somewhat frightened, not sure what to expect. As he looked her in the eyes, he once again broke down and started to cry. She looked shocked as he hugged her and kissed her on the cheek. "I'm so sorry, Mama," he said through the tears. "I'm the lowest person on earth. I've hurt you so bad, and all you've ever done is love me. Please forgive me. I'll never hurt you again. Never! Please forgive me!"

The two embraced for what seemed an eternity. Years of pain and resentment fell away as they stood hugging, forgiving each other.

We stayed at the church building until late in the evening, and the next night Alberto and his mother were back again. This time he brought seventeen of his friends with him. Many of them came forward that evening to accept Jesus as their Savior.

I still hear from Alberto from time to time. Today he is an active member and leader in another church. His life has been completely changed, thanks to Jesus.

A NEW HOPE

I praise God that he has allowed me to witness so many changed hearts and lives during my career. It's what keeps me fresh and excited about ministry. God has used my testimony to break some of the hardest hearts in the universe. And it works because I was once one of those hearts. I was so cold and angry and lost that no one on earth ever thought there was hope for me. But God knew differently.

When I look at someone like Alberto, I see myself as a boy. And when they look at me, they see hope. Hope that maybe they, too, can find their way out of the dungeon of nothingness. That is our connection. That is what God uses to reach them, as he reached me.

And nothing excites me more than to see these young people finally embrace that hope, embrace a new future. To see them put the past away forever. To see them lay their fears and anger at the feet of Jesus and start a new life.

That is the key to climbing out of the dungeon, the key to changing old habits and dead-end lifestyles, to leaving behind a life of sin for a future of holy living. The key is to lay it down, to let it go, to let the past be the past and look, instead, toward Jesus—toward the true future.

So many times people accept Jesus yet hang onto their past. They hear the language of forgiveness, but their hearts don't accept it, don't believe it. They can't imagine that what they have done no longer matters. They can't *feel* forgiven. So the chains remain. The sins of their past still linger, tempting them, beckoning them back. The ghosts of what they were still haunt them.

I see it every day. It's what causes people to backslide, to fall back into their old lifestyles. To seek out their old friends in a moment of weakness. To fall back into drugs and sex and sin.

It happens when people accept a new future without turning loose of the past. Without letting go of their guilt and remorse. Without forgiving themselves the way that Jesus has forgiven them. "I tell you, now is the time of God's favor," wrote the apostle Paul, "now is the day of salvation" (2 Corinthians 6:2).

It's not enough that we accept Jesus and ask for his forgiveness; we must also reject who we once were and completely embrace the new day— the day of our salvation. The day that our past is over. The day that our sins are no longer remembered by God, that nothing we've ever done matters anymore, that only the future remains. It needs to be more than a day of salvation; it needs to be a day of *transformation*. A day of new hope and new dreams—of a renewed heart, mind, and soul.

DEFEATING THE PRINCE OF THE PAST

Satan lives in the past. He is the prince of what once was, the king of regret and guilt. He lives to keep us there, to remind us of what we've done and how horrible we've been. His mind is consumed by thoughts of past victories; of the times he caused us to sin, to stumble, to fall for his lies. Because in his heart he knows that the past is all he has. When salvation comes, Satan's hold is over. And his only hope left is to make us *think* we are still captive. He can no longer have our souls, but he can make us miserable and ineffective as God's children.

Don't let him do it. Don't let him fill your mind with doubt and confusion, with thoughts of past sins—sins that God has chosen to forget. Sins that we need to forget before we can truly move forward.

That's what separates people like Alberto from so many others who accept Jesus. That's the difference between our Twelve Disciples and so many other kids who come to Christ. That's the difference between the masses who follow Christ and those few followers who live each day with a burning passion for Jesus! They have done more than accept salvation; they have *embraced* a completely new future. They have chosen to forgive themselves and look forward.

They look into the dungeon of nothingness and no longer see themselves; they see only those who are still trapped inside—those who need the salvation that they have found. And their hearts burn only with compassion, not regret.

Forgiveness is a gentle and tender kiss from heaven. It is God pressing his lips against a broken heart and kissing away the pain, the sorrow, the shame. Wiping away the hurt forever. He takes a heart filled with regret and replaces it with a new heart—one of hope and joy and love. One that beats strong and true to the music of heaven. One that has no past, only a bright and glorious future.

Let God kiss your heart and make it new. Don't live another day of regret. Don't let Satan steal another moment of your future by whispering forgotten memories into your ear.

Embrace your new heart and life in the arms of Jesus. Come to him. Let him take your ounce of faith and make you a new creation!

CHAPTER EIGHT

FROM THE MOON TO THE GHETTO

In my office I have a photo that is close to my heart. It's a picture of the late Col. Jim Irwin, one of the last astronauts to walk on the moon. He is standing on the moon, next to an American flag. On the photo Jim wrote, *To my brother, Nicky. From the depths of the ghetto, to the heights of the moon, Jesus has touched us and made us brothers! 29 July 1989.* Beneath it he signed, *Jim Irwin, Apollo 15.*

Jim was one of my dearest friends, a true brother in the Lord, and I miss him dearly. God brought us together many years ago to teach me an important lesson about living with passion. A different kind of passion.

Meeting an Astronaut

I met Jim when I was still living in North Carolina. Years ago, Gloria and I spent more than eight years in Raleigh, where we opened several centers for young girls—mostly runaways and pregnant teens without a place to live. Gloria loved it in Raleigh, and she wasn't happy to hear that God was calling me to Colorado Springs. It was a tough decision and a difficult time for our family, but the calling was very clear.

Jim somehow heard that we were moving to his hometown of Colorado Springs, so he called one day to welcome us as neighbors. I still remember how intimidating it was to talk with him on the phone for the first time. This was a man who had walked on the moon—a real astronaut. A living legend. And I was just a poor kid from Puerto Rico, a former gang leader turned evangelist. *What did I do to deserve such an honor?* I still don't know. But I'm glad he called, because it was the beginning of a long and beautiful friendship.

The first time Gloria and I had dinner with Jim and his wife, Mary, we could tell that we had a deep connection. We felt as if we had known them for years. Jim and Mary were so easy to be with, so loving and graceful. Gloria and Mary soon became the best of friends, and Jim and I couldn't get enough of each other. Couples pray for that kind of soul connection with other couples, but we never expected it would happen between us and such a legendary figure.

Those who followed Jim's career know that he was an avid outdoorsman and climber. I had never met anyone who loved the outdoors as he did. He had a passion for mountain climbing and had a goal of finding the remains of Noah's ark on Mount Ararat. He led several expeditions to Turkey to climb the mountain in search of the ark. His first attempt was in 1982. His team made it to the summit of Ararat and back, but they never saw the ark, though he was convinced it was there. In 1983 he led an aerial survey of the region yet still didn't find anything. He and I spent many hours talking about his quest, and I knew that his inability to see it for himself was one of his biggest disappointments in life.

Imagine a man who walked on the moon being discouraged about his accomplishments! But that's how Jim was. He was always reaching higher, always wanting to do more, to leave a greater legacy, to experience greater things in life. That's why I loved him so.

And he approached his faith the same way. No matter how much he did for the kingdom, he always wanted to do more, to reach more people, to be a more effective witness for Jesus. Everywhere he went he shared his faith, and he was never once intimidated. While I was in the ghetto witnessing to gang members, Jim was attending high-level dinners with presidents, kings, and diplomats. And he was doing the same thing we were doing—witnessing for Jesus. Wherever he traveled, he carried a stack of Bibles and passed them out at every opportunity. He once had a meeting with Mikhail Gorbachev, the president of the Soviet Union at that time, during the height of his popularity, and Jim spent the entire time talking about Jesus. He asked Gorbachev if he could pray with him and left him with a copy of the Bible. He was as bold a witness as anyone I've ever known.

Once Jim said to me, "I wish I could witness the way that you do," and his comment completely floored me. I looked at him and said, "Are you kidding? I wish I had your guts!"

FALLING OFF A MOUNTAIN

I remember scheduling a large crusade in Colorado Springs and asking Jim if he'd be willing to tell his testimony at the event. He gladly agreed, and we set a date. It was in 1982, and he was planning his first climb on Mount Ararat in Turkey, but he assured me that he'd be finished in time to be there.

Just days before the event, however, I learned that something had gone wrong with Jim's climb. No one seemed to know for sure what had happened, only that Jim had fallen during his descent and suffered massive injuries. I learned that Jim had been taken to a hospital in Turkey. I made numerous calls to find out how he was, to see if he was still alive, but I couldn't get much information. I was sick to my stomach at the thought of my friend being hurt.

Our crusade was held just three weeks after his accident, and I assumed that he wouldn't make it. But I'll never forget the day of the event. The coliseum was packed and I got up to speak; then suddenly, out of the corner of my eye, I noticed someone walking onto the stage toward me. I glanced over and couldn't believe my eyes! It was my friend Jim.

He had a huge bandage on the side of his head, and you could still see much of the damage to his scalp. I can't remember how many stitches he had, but they covered his head, and half of his hair had been shaved off. I couldn't help but laugh.

I stood at the microphone and said, "Ladies and gentleman, let me introduce Colonel Jim Irwin, the astronaut." He walked toward me, the large bandage protruding from the side of his head, the scar in full view of the audience. Suddenly he reached into his back pocket and pulled out a pair of scissors. Holding them high in the air he said, "I was just backstage cutting my hair, and I think I might have messed up." The crowd roared with laughter.

He spoke for about seven minutes, and the audience was mesmerized by his testimony. Jim was a powerful speaker, very soft spoken in person but dynamic in front of a crowd. Many came forward that evening to receive Christ—young people who today are lawyers, doctors, and leaders in their communities.

I remember watching him pray with those who came forward that evening. He cried with them and hugged them, sincerely hurting for those who needed Jesus. His heart was as big and genuine as the moon he had walked on.

A LONG WAY DOWN

So many times Jim would try to cajole me into climbing a mountain with him. I'd tell him, "I'm a runner, not a climber. I like to keep my feet on flat ground." But he stayed after me.

Then one day he knocked on my door at six in the morning, waking up my entire family. He stood on our porch in his running shorts and said, "Okay, Nicky. I've been after you for two years and now I'm not taking no for an answer. Today we're climbing Pikes Peak. Get your shorts on and meet me in the car!"

I thought he was kidding. "What are you talking about?" I said. "I told you I'm a runner, not a climber." We joked together, but it soon became clear that he wasn't going away. He was bent on getting me to climb Pikes Peak, and today was the day. So I threw on my shorts and went with him.

That climb turned into one of the most enjoyable days of my life. All the way up the mountain, Jim and I laughed and joked together. Several times we stopped to take in the beauty around us. We talked and prayed and shared many hidden thoughts and dreams. Jim shared some private things with me that were so special and transparent, things that I will take with me to the grave. Things that we will talk about again someday in heaven.

At around the halfway point, a thought suddenly hit me. "Jim," I asked, "how are we going to get down from the top? Do you have someone meeting us?"

"Don't worry," he answered. "I've got that all worked out."

Somehow he didn't sound convincing, but I let it go. Later I brought it up again. "Are you sure you have someone meeting us?" I asked. "It's a long way, and I really don't want to walk all the way down."

"Don't worry, Nicky. It's all arranged."

His Cheshire cat grin seemed to say otherwise, but again I let the matter drop. Rain clouds began to gather above us, and I worried about whether we would be able to beat them. By the time we reached the top, they had turned dark and black, into full-fledged storm clouds. I felt a few drops on my head. We quickly took pictures on top of the mountain, looked around a bit, said a brief prayer, and then I asked Jim, "So where is our ride?"

"Just follow me," he said.

He walked toward the road on the far side of the mountain and planted himself on one corner, where cars were passing by on the way down. Then he stuck out his thumb. I couldn't believe my eyes. He wanted us to hitchhike down the mountain!

"Are you nuts, Jim? I'm not going to hitchhike down!"

He gave me a big grin. "Okay, but it sure is a long walk. I guess I'll see you at the bottom."

I argued, but it didn't do any good. I offered to call Gloria, but it was already five in the afternoon, and by the time she reached us it would be well after dark. By now the rain had hit us full force, and it soon became clear that this was the only way down.

There we stood, the preacher and the astronaut, drenched from head to toe, with our thumbs in the air and our eyes pleading for a ride down the mountain. We were a sight to behold.

Nobody wanted to stop for us. We looked like a couple of homeless men, with our shorts and T-shirts, and our hair matted down from the rain. After a while Jim decided to get more aggressive. He saw a car coming and stepped in front of it. As the car stopped I looked inside and saw two women with panicked looks on their faces. The driver rolled her window down to see what Jim wanted, and when she saw Jim in his dirty T-shirt and running shorts, she quickly locked the door and rolled her window up. "Get away from me, you pervert," she screamed just before speeding away down the mountain. I laughed so hard that my side ached.

"Jim Irwin…the pervert astronaut," I called him. It became a running joke between us.

We finally hitched a ride with a young man in a pickup truck, but we had to ride in the back with his dog. It was a long, rough road, but we laughed and joked all the way down. It was one of the most memorable days of my life, and I will treasure it in my heart forever.

STRUCK DOWN TO EARTH

I was speaking in Ontario, California, when I got a frightening call from Gloria. She could barely get her words out. "Nicky, Jim had a heart attack," she told me through tears. I don't remember much more about the conversation, only that I immediately began making plans to fly back to Colorado the next day to see him.

I arrived at the hospital the next evening, but the nurses wouldn't let me in to see him. I tried to talk my way into his room, but they were adamant that only family was allowed. Gloria and I did our best to comfort Mary. "He's been asking for you," she told me.

Somehow Mary convinced the nurses to let me into Jim's room, and I wasn't prepared for what I saw. He was lying in bed with tubes running out of his body, helpless, white as a sheet, like a ghost. He was talking to the nurses but not making any sense. The pain of seeing my friend so weak and frail completely overcame me. I struggled to maintain my composure, mostly for Mary's sake. The heart attack had really taken its toll on his body.

Jim tried to jump out of bed when he saw me walk into the room. He was disoriented and thought I was there to go for a run with him. "Nicky," he said, "you're here to climb Pikes Peak with me. I'll be ready in a minute."

The nurses held him down and explained that he had to stay in bed. I held his hand and stood beside his bed. "We'll go climbing when you get well," I told him, fighting back tears. "You stay here and rest, Jim."

I prayed with him and stayed with him for a few minutes, then left so he could get some sleep. Seeing Jim in that hospital bed, like a lost little child, weak and sick and disoriented, is a memory that haunts me. He was always so full of life and energy, always moving and climbing and laughing. His sickness had sucked the energy out of him. In my heart I prayed that God would restore Jim to health and let him live a long time, but I sensed that his days on earth were coming quickly to an end.

LOSING A FRIEND

Several months later Jim was out of the hospital and doing better, though still weak and frail. The heart attack had done more damage than expected. He was still wired to a monitor and struggled to catch his breath. But his passion for the outdoors hadn't dwindled a bit. Over and over he reminded me of my promise to climb Pikes Peak with him again. "When you get better, Jim," I would tell him.

Finally I could hold him off no longer. He was adamant about wanting to make a climb, so I agreed to go with him—mostly to keep him from going alone and hurting himself.

We started slowly, one step at a time. Jim was still attached to a heart monitor, and I could hear the machine beeping and whizzing as we walked steadily up the mountain. Jim couldn't go far before stopping to rest. We would find a seat on a rock and just sit and talk and laugh, as we had done so many times before. The scenery was breathtaking, and Jim took it all in like a little child, as if seeing the beauty of God's creation for the very first time. "Look at the sun resting on the mountain," he'd say, with eyes wide as saucers. The next minute he'd be holding a flower in his hands, studying the petals with awe.

We shared so many private things that day. We shared our hearts, our failures, our regrets, our greatest joys. Several times we prayed together, thanking God for our friendship and for the blessings he had given us throughout our lives. It was as if Jim knew in his heart that this would be his last time on the mountain. As if he knew that God would soon be taking him home, and he wanted to first say good-bye to the mountain he loved and the friends he would be leaving behind.

We made it only halfway up the mountain before turning around and heading back down. I was surprised at how well Jim did, given his condition. Still, it was sad to see him struggle so much.

About five months later, in July 1991, I was speaking at a crusade on the East Coast when I learned that Jim had passed away. I quickly booked a flight back to Colorado. The day that Gloria and I went to the funeral home to be with Mary and pay our last respects to Jim was one of the most difficult times of my life. Jim wanted a closed-casket funeral, so only his family was able to see him, but Mary wanted Gloria and me alongside her. The pain of seeing my good friend in a coffin was unbearable. Seldom has my heart connected with another person as it had with Jim, and I cried tears of sadness as I stood over his body.

Mary asked me to speak at his funeral, and I agreed, though I wondered if I'd be able to get through it. The Irwins attended the same church as Gloria and I, Radiant Church, and I suggested that our pastor, Rev. Don Steiger, officiate the formalities. Mary thought that Jim would like that.

Gloria, Mary, and I were there alone with Jim. We cried and hugged each other. I leaned over and kissed Jim on the forehead one last time. "Thank you for the moment," I said to my friend.

SAYING GOOD-BYE

More than twelve hundred people came for Jim's funeral service the next day. I had never seen so many dignitaries and celebrities at a funeral before. There were senators and congressmen and numerous other political figures and celebrities. Ten of Jim's fellow astronauts were there to say good-bye to their friend. It seemed ironic that Jim was the last astronaut to go to the moon and yet the first of them to die. He was the first to make it to heaven. Jim had finally made it beyond the moon.

The church had to close the service to the media in order to keep it quiet. I've spoken at a number of funerals, but I've never had such a hard time getting my words to come out. I tried to make the occasion upbeat and humorous, as Jim would have wanted, but it was tough to overcome my sadness. I told of the many adventures Jim and I had shared together. The crowd laughed as I told them of our first climb up Pikes Peak and our hitchhiking ordeal down the mountain. I reminded them that Jim was not gone, only passed from this life to his eternal home, and that we would all be able to see him again some day. Yet in spite of my own words of encouragement, I struggled as much as anyone with Jim's death. It was all I could do to get through my eulogy.

I finished speaking and didn't feel like mingling with the crowd, so I slipped out the back door and went for a drive in my car. Black clouds hovered overhead, and rain drizzled from the sky as I drove through the lonely streets of the city, my wiper blades beating slowly in front of me. My heart felt as dark and gloomy as the weather. It was as if God were mourning with me, his tears raining down from heaven on those of us whom Jim had left behind.

As I drove, I didn't know whether I wanted to go home or to my office or to simply keep driving. I felt alone and aimless, agonizing over the loss of my friend. I began talking to God. "I miss Jim so much," I said. "I know there will be a day when Jesus will come again, when we will all go through a resurrection. I know I will see him again, and that we'll be together with you in heaven. But I'm so sad right now. Please help me get through this, God."

At that moment I sensed God speaking to my spirit. *Jim is in my hands now,* he said to me. *You will see him again. Those will be happier days. You'll be united once again.* It was a comforting thought—the only thing that got me through the evening.

When Jim died, a piece of me died with him. And I will always carry him with me in my heart.

A QUIET PASSION

God brought tremendous blessing into my life through my friendship with Jim Irwin, and he taught me a lot of lessons in the process. I learned what true friendship can be and how much we need people in our lives to share with, to minister with, and to relate to on a deep and meaningful level. Jim and I shared a connection of the soul. A connection of the heart and spirit.

We were brothers, spiritually and emotionally—two soul-obsessed believers, each just thrilled to be used for God's service.

Though I had been ministering to people my entire life, I learned more about evangelism from Jim than I could have learned from a thousand evangelistic crusades. He taught me that the best way to reach people is to simply love them. To laugh and cry with them. To smile with them and show them how much you care. To wrap them in your arms and call them your friends.

Jim had an infectious personality and a genuine love for people—all people. He never saw himself as a big-shot astronaut, just a simple man trying to live a good life. Though he was extremely bright and intellectual, he never intimidated people. He was extremely charismatic and approachable.

And how smooth he was! So suave and polished—completely the opposite of my personality. When it comes to sharing my faith, I'm something of an evangelistic "scrapper." I hold nothing back, and I can often come across as a bit intimidating. But Jim wasn't like that. He was smooth and nonconfrontational. He could charm anyone within minutes, and he shared his faith easily, calmly.

Many times I invited him to go with me to the inner city to witness, and he never let me down. He saw so many kids coming to Christ, and he always found time to sit and talk or pray with a teenager or a mother who was hurting. He had such genuine love and compassion for people—all people. He never looked down on another person, never saw himself as too good or important to give a helping hand to someone in need or a shoulder to cry on.

Jim allowed Christ to live through him. That was the secret to his effectiveness. That's why people loved him so much. And that's why I can't wait to get to heaven to climb another mountain with my good friend Jim by my side.

What Matters Most

History will remember Jim as the great astronaut who walked on the moon, but that's not how he'll be remembered in heaven. In heaven he'll be known as the quiet man who used his God-given influence to impact the lives of others. He'll be known as the spiritual father to many souls who found their way to heaven because of his humble spirit and his willingness to share his faith at every opportunity.

That's the greatest thing about following Jesus. You don't have to be rich or famous or even a great evangelist to make an impact on the world. You just have to be willing to let God use you. You just have to be available when God needs a servant to teach or touch or help another person in his name. You just have to be there. And any one of us can do that.

CHAPTER NINE

A QUIET MERCY

I t was the passion of Jesus that first attracted me to the faith. But it is his unfathomable mercy and compassion that keeps me mesmerized in his presence. When I read the stories of how he dealt with people during his time on earth, how he loved and cared for his disciples, how he healed and fed the masses that followed him, how he went to the cross to show his love for all mankind, I am left both humbled and dumbfounded by his grace.

Jesus is defined most clearly by the compassion he showed for others. And the goal of every Christian should be to live with that same kind of mercy and love. The kind of mercy that God shows his people each and every day. The kind of love that defies human understanding and logic.

That truth was brought home to me in the most powerful way many years ago, during a crusade in Poland.

A Beautiful Gift

The Communist regime was still in power at the time, at the height of its strength and popularity, and Poland was not friendly to outsiders who wanted to share their faith. Yet for some reason I was invited to speak there a number of times—even by the government. Something about my testimony touched them. The Communists knew of my background, and they seemed amazed that someone could rise out of the gutter the way I did. I knew it was only through the grace of Jesus that I was still alive, but they didn't understand such things. All they saw was a poor kid from the ghetto who made something of himself, and they were intrigued by that dynamic. In reality, God was simply working in their hearts, using my past to open their minds to the truth. And for my part, I welcomed the opportunity to teach them.

I'd heard so many stories of how cold and heartless the Communist leaders could be—and there was a lot of truth to that. But I always found them very open and warm. I sometimes wondered if it wasn't my Latino background that fascinated them. Or maybe the fact that I had been a gangster and a warlord. Whatever it was, it endeared me to them, and they treated me with nothing but respect whenever I went there to speak.

This one particular time, I had been invited by the mayor to speak in one of the largest coliseums in Poland. From the moment I arrived, I noticed several people following me wherever I went, three in particular. They were KGB agents. I found that with Communists, even when they liked you, they still struggled to trust you, so they always kept a close eye on visitors.

I noticed that one of them was a Cuban woman. They obviously wanted to make sure Gloria and I didn't share any secrets between us in Spanish. Everywhere we went, the three followed within earshot. They tried to be sneaky, but I was aware of them the entire time. I even joked with the woman about it once. I turned to her and said in Spanish, "I hope you're having a good time following us. Remember, Jesus loves you." I think I surprised her.

The night of the event, I couldn't believe how filled the stadium was when I arrived. Thousands of Polish citizens showed up for the event. The government expected me to give them a pep talk, to explain how I had risen out of poverty, and to perhaps encourage them to look at the bright side of life, in spite of their humble status and lack of food and clothing. But Jesus and I had other plans. I was going to share the gospel with every fiber of my being, holding nothing back. They wanted to know the secret to my success, and I fully intended to explain it. It was Jesus—not me!

Before going on stage, I took a few minutes alone to pray. "Jesus," I said, "I'm going to go out there tonight and talk of your love and forgiveness as never before. I'm going to witness for you as powerfully as I've ever witnessed. But I can't do it alone. I need your help. Only you can touch the hearts of these precious and lost people—only you can lead them to salvation. Use me, Lord! Help me share my heart and my testimony. Show them your grace and kindness."

That night I poured out my heart on stage. I told them that without Jesus I would probably have ended up dead in a gutter in the ghetto. That my life has no meaning and no hope without the love and mercy of God.

I told them of my days on the streets of New York, stealing for food and shelter, living day to day as an animal. I told them of the violence I had seen and inflicted upon others. Of the poverty and injustice within the inner city. And of the shame that I still felt because of the crime-ridden days of my youth.

Then I told of my mother, how she had spent most of her life enslaved by Satan and caught up in the world of the occult. How she had finally given her life to Jesus and changed her future forever. How she once served as a child of the devil yet ended her life in service to the one true God of the universe. How she was able to make such a powerful impact for Jesus during her last years on earth. How she had helped my father come to Jesus before the end of his life.

Then I told of the day that she and I had made peace with our past—the day that she had asked my forgiveness for the abuse and neglect she had inflicted upon me during my childhood. The day that I forgave her and prayed with her as she accepted Jesus as her Savior. The day that Jesus forever broke our family curse.

When I finished, I pleaded with them to give their lives to Jesus. "You know what poverty is like," I told them. "So many of you are living today as I did so many years ago. You're lonely and afraid. You don't always know where your next meal is coming from. You feel like an animal, living aimlessly from day to day. But life doesn't have to be that way. Let Jesus give you purpose. Let him give you a reason to live, a reason to go on living. Let him come into your heart and change it forever—to give you a new heart and a new mind. A new direction. Let Jesus save you!"

The man who translated for me that day was an extremely educated Polish man, a scientist, and I could tell he was having a hard time staying focused. Several times I looked over at him and saw tears in the corners of his eyes. He did his best to stay composed, but as I told the story of my mother, we had to stop. He bent over and began crying uncontrollably. It was an awkward moment, and I wasn't sure what to do.

I took a step toward him and placed my hand on his shoulder. "Are you okay?" I asked. He said to me, "I've never heard such a story of forgiveness before. I'm sorry, Nicky. I'll be all right in a minute."

The stadium grew deathly quiet. People were so moved by the interpreter's response that many started crying. It was the first time I can remember having to stop a service so that the translator could compose himself. His response so touched my heart that I started crying with him. For the longest time we stood on the stage in silence. After a few minutes I patted him on the back and whispered, "We need to finish. Will you be able to go on?" He wiped his eyes and nodded, then continued translating.

I invited people to come forward and accept Jesus, and no one was prepared for the response. Like a tidal wave, the Spirit of the Lord crashed upon the crowd, bringing people to conviction. The translator's brokenness had resonated with the crowd. God used his heart to bring a spirit of brokenness to the crowd. All over the stadium people began flooding the aisles to come forward. Every direction I looked, masses were moving toward us. Few times have I experienced such a show of remorse and repentance from a crowd of people. Such urgency! Such sorrow and shame! People were in tears, pushing their way toward the front. I knew that they were responding to the translator's heartfelt tears as much as to my testimony. He was the anointed one that evening.

So many people were coming that I wondered if they'd understood what I had asked. "I want everyone to stop for just a moment," I said. "Wherever you are, stand still for a few seconds."

I waited until the crowd stopped before continuing. "I want to make sure you understand the commitment you are making by coming forward," I said. "I'm not asking you to come if you feel sorry; I'm asking if you want to turn your life over to Jesus. I'm talking about completely opening up your heart and soul to God. This is a lifetime commitment you are making. Jesus wants you to turn away from sin for the rest of your life. Don't come if you're not ready to do that. Don't come to impress your friends or to make me feel good. Come only if you're willing to give God the rest of your life—to change the way you live—to give your heart completely to Jesus."

I again invited them to come, and no one sat down. People came from every corner of the coliseum. Half the seats were empty. It was the most powerful altar call I had ever experienced.

More than ten thousand people attended the event that day, and more than six thousand of them came forward for conversion. The few workers we had were completely overwhelmed, and we stayed long into the evening hours trying to minister to them all. It was a powerful evening in the presence of God. The Holy Spirit had worked mightily in the hearts of those who had come.

I was floating on air through the entire ordeal. There's nothing that brings more joy to my heart than seeing people give up their lives and come to Jesus. Nothing fills my life with greater pleasure.

Thank you, Jesus, I prayed silently. *Thank you for such a powerful display of your love and forgiveness. Thank you for working so mightily among us.*

I was so moved by the interpreter's response that I later went with him to the park to talk. I couldn't believe what a sweet, genuine person he was, so gentle and warm. A godly man. He told me how much he loved the Lord and how hard it was to live in Poland under the persecution of the government. He told me how my testimony had moved him. At one point he grew quiet and motioned toward the KGB agents following us. "That's why I can't talk to you much," he whispered. "I can never share what's really on my heart." It broke my heart to see him in such pain—to have to live under such scrutiny and bondage.

Before I left Poland, two of the KGB agents approached me to talk about the Lord. I was surprised that they came to me in public, but they wanted to know more about Jesus, so I told them. Right in the open I prayed with them and led them to salvation. I'll never forget how excited they were. "Thank you," they kept telling me.

Still today I remember that trip as one of the greatest highlights of my ministry—one of the most precious times of evangelism I've ever experienced. It was as if God was giving me a gift that I could always cherish.

A gift, perhaps meant to lighten the blow of what was about to happen.

UNWELCOME NEWS

I awoke early the morning after my crusade, still floating on a cloud of excitement, and decided to go for a run through the streets of Poland. I put on my jogging clothes and slipped my Walkman headphones over my ears. I went down the elevator, out the front door of the hotel, and started down the street. The morning was crisp and beautiful and lively. The cool air felt good against my face as I ran through the dirty, unkempt streets toward the edge of the city.

My plan was to run about twelve miles—my usual workout—but around the fourth mile I got a sudden catch in my spirit. I sensed God calling to me, wanting to speak. I slipped the headphones around my neck and began to pray. *Is there something you need me to know, Jesus?*

For a while I heard nothing, sensed nothing, and wondered if I was just getting carried away with the excitement of the previous night. So I continued to run and enjoy the scenery. Then suddenly, the feeling came again. My spirit felt uneasy, and I wondered if God was trying to give me a message. I continued to run and pray and meditate. Suddenly I said to God in my spirit, *Are you going to take my mother, Lord? Is it her time to go?*

Even as the thought left my mind, I sensed God speaking to my spirit. *Yes, Nicky, I'm taking your mother away. I'm taking her home to be with me. It's time for her to rest.*

Tears started pouring down my cheeks. The sadness completely overwhelmed me, and I couldn't stop crying. I cut my run short and headed back to the hotel to tell Gloria what I had sensed the Lord telling me.

My mother was living in Connecticut at the time, and I immediately called my brother to ask how she was. "Mother is not doing well," he told me. "You should come home to see her."

I remember pleading with the Lord to please let me see my mother before she died. I had received a telegram from my brother saying that she had been asking for me, and I couldn't bear the thought of her departing without seeing her one more time. I told God, "I know I need to stay and finish my work here, but please don't let my mother pass until I see her." But he didn't give me an answer.

I finished my crusade in Poland and then quickly booked a flight back to New York. The flight was delayed by several hours, and I continued to worry that I wouldn't make it home in time. Satan was working overtime to keep me from seeing her. We finally boarded the plane to London, but time was slipping away quickly.

I arrived in New York late the next evening and immediately called my brother to pick me up and take me to Connecticut. "She's still asking for you, Nicky," he said. "You need to hurry if you want to see her. I don't think she'll last long." I still had hopes that I'd make it in time. God had still not given me a clear answer to my prayer.

But it wasn't to be. Mother died that evening before I reached her home. She passed away just a few hours before I arrived. Though I was sad that I didn't get to say good-bye, I knew in my heart that she was in good hands. God had put a peace in my spirit. Mama was with Jesus. I still don't understand why God didn't allow me to see her, but I know he had his reasons. I simply released her into his hands, knowing that her soul was secure. And that was all the comfort I needed.

A Final Trip

As difficult as it was to bury my mother, I found myself completely overwhelmed by the tenderness God showed me through the process. Not only did he give me a word of comfort in my spirit beforehand, preparing me for her death, but he ministered to me throughout the dark days surrounding her funeral. In the midst of my sadness I felt an indescribable calmness in my heart. Knowing that she was with the Lord, dancing with the angels, reuniting with my father, resting in the arms of Jesus filled my soul with joy.

I remembered the time that we almost lost her, more than twenty-five years earlier, before she knew the Lord, and I praised God for extending her life, giving her many more years to serve him. I thought back to the days that we were able to pray and laugh together, rejoicing in our newfound life in Jesus, rebuilding the years of abuse and hate from my childhood—the years that Satan had stolen from us.

How could I possibly thank Jesus enough for what he had given us? Any sorrow I experienced paled in comparison to the gratitude I felt toward God. Knowing that my mother was in heaven was all I needed or wanted.

I bought her the nicest coffin I could find and purchased a ticket to fly her back with me to Puerto Rico, so that she could be buried in her homeland. It was our last trip together. I sat in the airplane while mother rested in the belly of the plane, among the suitcases. It was a sad and introspective flight for me. I spent much of the time talking to my mother, hoping that her spirit could hear me. "This is our last trip together," I told her. "I'm going to miss you so much. Thank you for being such a wonderful mother. The last years have been so precious to me. I thank God that he came into your heart and brought us back together again. We had so many good times together. I love you so much, Mama. And I'll see you soon in heaven."

CRAWLING INTO THE HEART OF CHRIST

When I think of how tender and compassionate God was to me during that time it brings tears to my eyes. At a time when I most needed comfort, he was right there beside me, holding me, whispering in my ear, *Don't worry, Nicky. Your mother is with me.* I found greater shelter and solace in the arms of God than I could have ever found on earth.

In my hour of need, I crawled into the heart of Christ, and he embraced me, as he has always done during dark and lonely moments. This is the relationship I have with Jesus. It is how he lets me know how much he cares for me—how he cares for all those who depend on him. For those who love him and accept him as their Brother.

It reminds me of when my children were very small. There were times when they would be playing on the carpet and they would hurt their finger on a toy. They'd start to cry, and I would go over to see what happened. I'd bend down and extend my arms. "Come see daddy. Let me kiss the hurt," I'd say.

They would immediately crawl toward me and let me pick them up onto my lap, and then I would hold them, kiss them, comfort them.

"Don't worry," I'd whisper softly into their ear. "Daddy is here. Everything will be all right."

At these moments, I wouldn't just hold them; I would fold them into my heart. They could feel the love I had for them, a love that only a father can feel for his babies. A love that goes beyond explanation. A love that is real and eternal and unconditional. A love that knows no limits.

That's how God sees his children. When we hurt, he stands with arms extended in our direction, saying, "Come see Daddy. Let me kiss the hurt." All we have to do is crawl into the heart of God, and everything will be all right. We have complete access by his Spirit. He loves us as only a Father could love his children.

That's the kind of relationship he wants each of us to have with him. That's the kind of God we serve. His compassion runs deep and wide and knows no limits. His love is as real and vibrant as the morning mist or the evening sky. "In you, O LORD, I have taken refuge," David wrote. "Be my rock of refuge, to which I can always go.... From birth I have relied on you; you brought me forth from my mother's womb. I will ever praise you" (Psalm 71:1,3,6).

David understood that without God's mercy and compassion his life would not be worth living. He didn't just serve the God of the universe; he had a real relationship with a loving and gracious Father. That's what set him apart from other kings and Jews of the day. That's what endeared him to God so powerfully.

And that's how God wants all of his children to see him.

Know God for his power and might, but define him by his love and mercy. Because that's how he most wants us to see him.

CHAPTER TEN

REFLECTIONS OF JESUS

I probably wouldn't have noticed Jamie if she hadn't been standing in the middle of so many men in front of the stage. She was young, about fifteen, and her head was bowed slightly, her eyes cast downward toward the ground. Her mother stood behind her. I sensed that the young girl had been forced to come that evening. You could see in her eyes that she didn't want to be there.

I had just finished giving an altar call at a citywide event in Houston, Texas, and that evening I had talked of the manhood of Jesus. I told the crowd that Jesus was a "man's man," not a wimp, as he is so often portrayed. Before coming to Christ I thought I knew what it meant to be tough, but I didn't. Inside I was a frightened child. But Jesus taught me how to take responsibility for my actions, how to be a real man. I peeled off the "wimpy" label we tend to put on Jesus, and the message resonated with the crowd—especially the men in the audience. That's why my altar call had convicted so many men to accept Jesus as their Savior or to rededicate themselves to God.

And that's why Jamie stood out so starkly. She was young and beautiful. And I could tell she was hurting. I had trouble reading her expression. When she glanced in my direction, her eyes seemed hollow, cold, distant. She looked angry and embarrassed at the same time. And it was obvious she didn't trust me.

I took a few steps forward and stood face to face with her. She glanced upward, and I noticed bruises around her cheeks and eyes—bruises that she had tried to hide with makeup. "Your father beat you, didn't he?" I asked her. The question came out of nowhere; I wasn't even thinking about it before it came out of my mouth. It was the Holy Spirit who put the thought in my mind.

She didn't answer, just stood staring at me, her eyes cold and lifeless. So I asked again. "Tell me, did your father beat you?"

"Yes," she said abruptly, anger exploding from her eyes. "My father beat me up unmercifully. And he is a Christian!"

Her words were meant to cut and accuse, and they succeeded on both counts. I felt horrible. For several seconds I didn't know what to say. I wanted to explain to her that no true Christian man would do such a thing, that if her father were a true follower of Christ, he could never inflict such harm to his child. But I knew my words would be falling on deaf ears. So I held my tongue.

"I'm so sorry he beat you," I said to her softly. "I know you're hurting. Can I pray for you?"

At that moment her face softened and her lips began to quiver. Her eyes turned red, and she began to cry, slowly, softly. I moved closer and put my hand on her shoulder. Then her tears flowed, as if a dam had burst in her eyes. She rested her face on my shoulder as I prayed for her.

I later learned that her father was a nominal Christian who only attended church occasionally. Jamie's mother claimed that she knew nothing of the abuse, but I was certain that she did. How could a mother not know such a thing?

Jamie came that night only because her mother forced her. And I'm still not sure what forces brought her forward to see me. Only that God had been working in her heart, moving in her spirit, trying to help heal her wounded soul.

When I finished praying, Jamie wiped her eyes with the sleeve of her shirt. She smiled at me, and for the first time her face seemed calm. Soft. Almost loving. "Thank you for praying for me," she said. "I know Jesus will get me through this."

I hugged her again and encouraged her to forgive her father and move forward. "Let Jesus be the Father you need," I told her. "He won't ever let you down." In my heart I prayed that Jamie would be able to move past the abuse and pain and that the scars inflicted by her father would not define her future. But in my mind I struggled with deep feelings of anger toward this man I had never met. This man who pretended to follow Christ while terrorizing his little girl. This coward who has done more harm to his family than he probably will ever realize.

The Pain of Hypocrisy

I will never understand how some people can claim Jesus as their Savior yet live as if they had never experienced his saving grace. How they can ask God to redeem them while living unrepentant, unremorseful lives. How they can talk as if they know Christ when their actions show clearly that they know nothing about him.

These kinds of people do more harm for the kingdom than Satan could ever hope to accomplish. They are the Enemy's greatest allies in a world that already looks for ways to discount the claims of Christ. Paul tells us, "Do not conform any longer to the pattern of this world, but be transformed by the renewing of your mind" (Romans 12:2). For too long Christians have conformed to the ways of the world. We have allowed the world to not only *affect* us but to completely *infect* us. To take over our hearts and minds and keep us in bondage to sin, even though we convince ourselves that we're free.

But Jesus promises to bring transformation to our hearts and minds, to renew us, to change the way we think and live and act. If we have not allowed him to do that, we have not really accepted him.

"Create in me a pure heart, O God," wrote David, "and renew a steadfast spirit within me" (Psalm 51:10). These words should epitomize the desire of every follower of Christ. It should be our prayer daily. To ask God for a new heart and a new mind, to plead for a pure life, to strive moment by moment to live with greater mercy and grace and innocence. To become more like Jesus with each passing day.

When the world looks at us, what they see will define their view of God. It will shape how they perceive our heavenly Father, what they think of him, how they come to understand his goodness and grace. We are ambassadors for the kingdom in a lost and fallen world. And our actions, both good and bad, will reflect directly on God.

Jamie's father claimed to know Jesus, and in doing so he became her spiritual point of reference. She saw how he treated his family and projected those attributes onto God. Every time she looked at him, her view of God was being shaped and molded. When he beat her, she felt as if God were the one leveling the blows. When he screamed at her, it was God's voice that she heard.

And today, because of her father, because of this coward of a man, Jamie will struggle for the rest of her life to trust God.

MY FIRST CHURCH SERVICE

I had been a Christian for only four days when I encountered this same type of hypocrisy in the church. And it could have easily caused me to fall away.

Right on the heels of my conversion, a pastor invited me to his church. I was so on fire for the Lord that I counted the moments leading up to the service. I couldn't wait to get to church. I was in love with Jesus, and all I wanted to do was worship him, sing to him, hear about him some more. I was thrilled at the thought of making new friends—Christian friends, who understood my new faith.

By the time Sunday rolled around I had convinced more than fifty of my gang friends to go with me. They couldn't believe I was serious, but I wouldn't take no for an answer. Israel was the leader of the gang at that time, and I woke him up early Sunday morning to remind him. "We're going to church, Israel," I said. "Get everyone together; we don't want to be late."

That evening our group took up much of the auditorium. We looked completely out of place, and I think a lot of the people were afraid of us. I remember being aware of how intimidating we must have looked, a bunch of Latino gangsters spread out over a large section of the sanctuary.

Most of my friends didn't know how to act in church. I didn't know either, but I knew we were supposed to show some sense of order and reverence. I remember Tico, one of our gangsters, smooching on his girlfriend at the end of the row behind me. He was all over her, kissing and hugging her. The service had just started, and the pastor came over and whispered into my ear, "Nicky, would you do me a favor?"

I perked up. "Sure, pastor. What's in your skin?"

He looked surprised. I'm not sure he understood our ghetto lingo.

"I'm glad you and your friends are here," he told me, "but your friend really shouldn't be doing that in church. This is God's house, and your friend is upsetting people. I know he doesn't mean any harm, but people here don't understand that you come from a different world. Could you talk to your friend and ask him not to do that?"

I was embarrassed and did my best to apologize. "I'll take care of it. I'm sorry."

I got up and walked around the aisle to where Tico was sitting and said to him, "Tico, I know you're a romantic person, but some of the people are offended by the way you're behaving. Why don't you take your girl-friend outside for about five minutes, and you can kiss her all you want. Then come back when you're done and sit down."

Tico seemed confused, but he agreed. "No problem," he said with a big grin. The two left and were gone for about twenty minutes. They later came back into the auditorium and slipped into their seats. Tico must have gotten it out of his system, because he had a huge grin on his face. Several times he looked at me with his head bobbing, giving me the thumbs-up sign. He sat still through the rest of the service.

During the altar call, both Tico and his girlfriend went forward to receive Christ. And so did many others who had come with me. I could hardly contain my excitement. Not only had Jesus changed my life, but he was changing the lives of my gang friends as well. It was one of the most exciting moments of my life, seeing so many of my gang friends kneeling at the altar, praying to receive Jesus as their Lord and Savior.

And it almost didn't happen. We almost left the building that evening before the service even started. All because of an event that happened just a few hours earlier.

A Discouraging Encounter

We had arrived at the church building early that morning, and the first person we ran across was an older woman. She was standing outside the front door, looking at us with disdain as we walked up the steps to the building. As soon as I reached the top step, she said to me, "What are you doing here with that long hair, you sinner?"

Her words took me back. I tried to talk calmly to her. "We're just here to honor the pastor," I told her. "He invited us to come."

"Well you don't belong here," she snapped. "You need to cut your hair."

I couldn't believe my ears. Immediately my defenses rose to the surface. "What, is this a barbershop?" I asked. "I thought it was a church building!"

My friends laughed aloud, but the woman wasn't amused in the least. "And just look at the way you walk," she said. "Can't you walk straight?"

I was stunned. Her arrogance dumbfounded me—not to mention her guts. Here we were, more than fifty hardened gangsters, and this old woman was taunting us. She had no idea what I would have done to her just a week earlier—and what my friends would have done if I hadn't been there to stop them.

"What's wrong with the way I walk? What do you want me to do… walk like a girl?" Again my friends laughed, but the woman remained stern and defiant.

"You just don't belong here," she snapped angrily before turning to walk into the building. For several minutes my friends howled on the front steps of the church building as I contemplated what to do. I was embarrassed that they had witnessed such a scene. I wanted this to be a good experience for them. I had brought them in hopes of reaching them for Jesus, and I couldn't believe that this was the first experience they had in church—that this was my first experience in church.

I also feared what they might do. That woman had no idea how dangerous my gang could be. They would have torn the place apart if I hadn't done something to calm them down. "Don't worry about her," I told them. "This isn't her church; it's the pastor's church. We're here to honor him, not her. Forget about her." The woman never knew that I probably saved her life that night.

Quite honestly, I seriously considered just leaving and not coming back. But something in my spirit told me not to get discouraged. That this poor woman didn't reflect the Jesus that I had come to serve. I wanted to believe that my newfound faith was not a lie. So I summoned the courage to put the incident behind me and walk into the building.

I thank Jesus that I did. Who knows how things might have turned out in my life—and the lives of many of my friends—had I allowed this bitter old woman to define my view of God?

ANOTHER ATTACK BY SATAN

Satan wasn't through trying to discourage us that evening. When the service was over, after watching so many of my gang friends accept Jesus, we left the church building and walked into a big surprise.

I walked out the front door of the building to see a handful of rival gang members waiting for us across the street. Somehow they had found out that we were in church and came to jump us. Several of them had guns aimed in our direction.

At that instant, I turned to see the woman who had confronted us earlier, walking out the door behind me. I grabbed her and pushed her back inside the building just before a shot rang out and hit the building. It was the second time I had saved her life that evening.

We ducked back into the church building and crouched down behind the door, wondering how we were going to get out. Shots were ringing out all around us. The other gang knew that we probably didn't have any weapons with us, so they waited for us to make a run for it.

Luckily, someone called the police that evening, because they showed up within a few minutes. The other gang took off down the street just before the police pulled up in front of the building. No one was hurt, but it could have been a bloody confrontation.

I walked home that evening by myself, with nothing in my hands but a Bible—my new, thick Bible that I cherished so much. I was in such a good mood, so thankful to Jesus for what he had done. I prayed and thanked him as I walked. Then out of nowhere another gang member jumped me and sliced my right hand with his knife. He ran and I instinctively chased after him. My anger flared and my legs carried me so fast that I caught up with him quickly, throwing him against a car. I fought the knife out of his hands, causing him to drop it beneath the curb.

I reached over and snapped the antenna off the car—one of the many tricks I had learned on the streets. If you don't have a weapon, you use what you can. I grabbed him by the throat and held him against the car, the point of the antenna just inches away from his eyes. I knew I had him. Just a quick flip of my wrist and he'd never bother me again. Everything inside of me wanted to hurt him for good, to get back at him for jumping me and slicing my hand. Blood ran down my right arm and all over the front of my clothes.

But I couldn't do it. Something inside of me kept saying, *Nicky, let him go. This isn't you anymore. This isn't your life. This isn't what Jesus saved you for.* I wanted to hurt him so bad, but Jesus wouldn't let me do it. My new heart wouldn't let me do it.

I dropped the antenna to my side and turned loose of him. "Go on. Get out of here," I said. He looked at me in shock, then took off down the street as fast as his legs could carry him.

For the first time in my life, I had chosen forgiveness over retaliation. And it felt really good. Better than anything I had ever experienced!

REFLECTING CHRIST

Paul told the Colossians, "Therefore, as God's chosen people, holy and dearly loved, clothe yourselves with compassion, kindness, humility, gentleness and patience.... And over all these virtues put on love, which binds them all together in perfect unity" (Colossians 3:12,14). There is a reason we are called to live as Christ lived. Because the world will look at our lives, at the way we live, at the things we say and do, and reflect those images onto Jesus. They will see him as they see us. Nothing brings greater disgrace to the cause of Christ than people who claim to know him but live in anger and judgment and arrogance. People who live in sin and hypocrisy within the church.

And the reverse is also true. Nothing brings greater honor to Christ than people who exude a lifestyle of love and compassion and kindness.

People who see others as Jesus sees them and treat other people the way that Jesus would treat them. People who live as Christ would live.

Every day you and I have to make that choice. It is already a given that our actions will reflect on Jesus, but what we reflect is a decision we have to make. A decision we make day by day, hour by hour, minute by minute. Will we choose to live in grace and kindness and mercy? Or will we live in bitterness and hypocrisy?

What we decide makes all the difference in how the world reacts to God's message of hope and salvation.

CHAPTER ELEVEN

CHILDREN OF THE VALLEY

M y children didn't grow up in the same kind of household in which I was raised. They know nothing of the kind of neglect and abuse and hate that I struggled with daily during my childhood. Even when I tell them the stories of my youth, they have a hard time believing the stories much less understanding them.

Our social status is completely different. I grew up in severe poverty while they grew up relatively comfortable. God has blessed our ministry through the years, and though we were never rich, we always had more than we needed. My children grew up in a house filled with love and laughter and kindness. I grew up feeling worthless and unwanted, without so much as a hug from my mother. They grew up surrounded by friends who loved and respected us. I grew up cowering in shame, hearing the whispers behind my back as I passed people in the streets, hiding from the stares of strangers as they drove by to get a glimpse of the evil Spirit House. They spent their teenage years laughing and playing with friends in a good school. I spent mine alone, trying to survive in the cold streets of Brooklyn.

It's often hard for me to imagine the life I once lived. I see the gangs in the ghetto and can't fathom myself living in such hopelessness and despair, living without Jesus in my life. Yet I have no trouble remembering the days that I did. Remembering my life as an angry and abused child in Puerto Rico. My days of wandering the streets of New York, fighting for respect and stealing for my next meal. My days of senseless hate and violence as a warlord of the infamous Mau Maus.

My children can't comprehend my past because it is so different from theirs.

And though the memories are still painful, I never want to forget. No matter how good things get in my life, no matter how many years pass, no matter how much my life changes, I intend to remember my days in the valley of despair. Because only through remembering where I've been can I fully appreciate what God has done for me.

Too often Christians make their way to the mountaintop without ever looking back at the valley. We're so caught up in the climb that we forget how far we've come. We forget our days of bondage and misery before Jesus set us free. Our moments of helplessness and despair. Our nights of emptiness and pain.

We forget that others are still caught in the world that we left behind.

One of the reasons I continued to take my children on our crusades in the ghettos when they were young is so that they would grow up appreciating their lives of freedom in Christ. I wanted them to see what it looked like to live a life void of Jesus. A life of hopelessness and bondage. I wanted them to experience a side of life that they knew nothing about. I wanted them to learn compassion for the lost by witnessing firsthand the emptiness of living without Jesus. I wanted my children to have a soul obsession in the depths of their hearts, so I allowed them to see the helplessness that comes with being lost to sin.

From Heaven to the Valley

Jesus chose to be a child of the valley. Before he came to earth he was living in greater glory than we could possibly imagine. The Son of the King of the universe. He sat at the right hand of God. He *is* God. And yet he chose to step down from his throne and enter the world of the valley. He chose to live among the hopeless and lost of creation. He humbled himself, denied himself, emptied himself for our sake. And he went to the cross in shame to create a bridge between the valley and the mountaintop.

The valley is a cold and heartless place to live. It is defined by blindness and drought and hunger. You can feel the rejection, the hurt, the insecurity. The fear. The turmoil. You can smell the hopelessness and pain. You can sense the anguish and sorrow. And the valley has nothing to do with income or social status. It's a state of the heart. It is anyplace apart from knowing and trusting God.

Valley people are everywhere you look. I see them living in penthouses in Manhattan, in nice suburban homes, and in broken-down shacks in the ghetto. Where they live makes no difference. Their lives are just as lost and lonely. Their hearts are frightened and alone. Their souls hunger for something more, something greater, something meaningful. They long for Jesus, though they don't know it.

Jesus came to the valley to bring hope and love and compassion, to bring sight to the blind, to show the way out. He came to bring new life to those who were dead. He went to the valley because that's where the lost people lived. And yet, so often, those he sets free never take the time to look back. They never make an effort to journey back into the valley to help others find their way out. They never travel into the valley of hopelessness to bring hope.

A STORY FROM THE VALLEY

I'm convinced that the reason most Christians steer clear of the valley is that they haven't felt the joy of leading others to freedom. If they could see what I've seen, experience what we all experience in our crusades, they would be obsessed with saving souls.

I wish they could have been standing beside me when I first met Manny.

Manny was seventeen when he came to one of our *Run Baby Run* crusades in Harlem in 1999. *Run Baby Run* is a play that depicts my childhood and my days of living in the streets of Brooklyn. It is a graphic display of what gang life is all about, showing the violence and helplessness of life in the ghetto.

Manny only came that evening because he had a free ticket from one of our Hit 'n' Run outreaches, and I'm sure he wasn't prepared for how the evening would affect him. His life had been defined by chaos and turmoil, and the play hit much closer to home than he expected. At the end of the play, I gave my testimony, then encouraged people to come forward if they wanted to accept Jesus.

Something brought Manny forward that evening. Hundreds came to the front for prayer, many drenched in tears of sorrow and repentance, but not Manny. He was stern-faced and rigid. A hard kid. An angry kid. He stood to one side with his hands in his pockets and his eyes cast downward.

Our TRUCE workers were busy praying for the many people who had come forward, doing their best to reach all of them, yet no one ventured near Manny. He looked tough and frightening, wearing gang colors, with no hint of emotion on his face.

I noticed him out of the corner of my eye. He looked completely out of place at an altar call—the last kid you would ever expect to come forward for help. Yet I see it all the time. It is the kids who look the toughest, who seem the hardest, who are the most frightened and lonely inside. They want desperately to open up, to share their misery, yet they don't know how.

I could tell Manny was surprised when I walked over and stood in front of him. I didn't speak, just looked him in the eye. He glanced at me, then quickly looked away. But he didn't move. His face remained cold and stern.

I reached my arms around his large shoulders and pulled him toward me, burying his head in my chest. His muscles tightened, but he didn't resist. Without warning he began to cry. His body was still stiff, but his tears drenched the front of my shirt.

I whispered into his ear, "You're hurting, aren't you?"

With that he began to sob even deeper. His muscles went limp and a flood of tears burst loose. I could literally feel his pain with each new tear.

"I've been running for so many years," he said finally, still weeping. "I'm so tired of running. You say God forgave you, but there's no way he could forgive me. Not for what I've done."

I lifted Manny's head from my shoulder and looked him in the eyes. "Tell me what you've done," I said.

Without pause, he began to tell me of the hate and violence he had lived through. The things he had done that shamed him. The pain he had been through and inflicted on others. Then he told me of his childhood.

"When I was a little boy, I came home from school one day and started looking around the apartment for my mother. I was hungry, and I couldn't find her anywhere. Suddenly my dad grabbed me by the throat and threw me against the wall. I couldn't figure out why he was mad. I asked him what I did wrong, but he didn't say anything. He had a gun, and he pointed it at my head. 'I'm going to kill you right now,' he told me.

"I begged him to put the gun away. I asked him over and over, 'What did I do, Dad? Why are you acting like this?' But he wouldn't answer me. He just kept waving the gun at me, saying, 'I'm going to kill you right now!'

"I was so scared. I wanted to run, but I knew he could catch me. I didn't know what to do. Then all at once he turned the gun on himself and said, 'I've changed my mind. I'm going to just kill myself.' I screamed at him, 'No, Dad. Don't do it!' But he did. He shot himself in the head. The gun dropped, and he fell backward onto the floor. Blood was everywhere. I froze. I was so scared, and I didn't know what to do. I felt water running down my pants leg, and I couldn't move. I screamed at him, 'Why, Dad? Why did you do it? Daddy! Daddy…' But he was gone.

"I don't know how long I stood there crying before Mama came home. She screamed and ran over toward Daddy, lying on the floor bleeding. He wasn't breathing. She kept asking me, 'What happened? Why did he do this?' But I couldn't answer her. 'Daddy's gone,' I said, over and over. 'Daddy's gone.'"

Finally Set Free

Manny buried his head into my shoulder once again. I held him tightly. "I can't get rid of the nightmares," he sobbed. "It's been so long, and they won't go away. Every night I see him lying on the floor, blood gushing from his head. And the nightmares are only getting stronger! I can't sleep, and I'm afraid to go to bed every night! Why did he do that? Why did he leave us? What did I do wrong? I hate him for leaving us! I hate him!"

I embraced Manny even tighter, holding his head in my chest. My heart ached for him. At first I didn't know what to say. He was so young and angry and confused. *What could I possibly say to take away the pain of such a horrible experience?*

"I understand," I told him. "I know what you're going through. I've had nightmares too. I know how horrible they can be. I understand the hell you're going through. The devil has painted this picture in your mind, and he keeps bringing it back to haunt you. But Jesus can take it away. Let him help you get rid of the pain!"

For several minutes I just held him as he cried. All I knew to do for Manny was to embrace him, to embrace his pain, to try my best to comfort him. I wanted to be the father that he had lost, if only for a moment. So I did what I know Jesus would have done. I held him.

Tears from the deepest corner of his soul cried out in agony—tears that had been buried for so many years. "I had so many horrible paintings in my head," I continued. "So many things I had done. So much violence I had witnessed. But now they don't haunt me anymore. If you ask God, he will take them away. Accept him into your heart and let him start healing you. Let him help you get free of your life of pain and violence. Let him help you forgive your father, so you can move forward. You have so many years to live—so much to live for. Don't lose another day. Don't let Satan steal any more of your life. You can't change the past, but you can change your future. You can start over! Accept Jesus, and let him help you start over again!"

Manny lifted his head from my chest and again fixed his gaze squarely. For the first time I could see his eyes lighten. He looked like a little child.

"Do you really think he will do that?" he asked me. "Will he really accept me, after all I've done?"

"Of course he will," I told him. "He's begging you to come to him. God has been watching you all your life. He knows the pain you've been through. He understands your struggle, more than you could ever imagine. He's calling you to accept him—to accept Jesus and change your life forever."

I prayed with Manny, and he repeated each word. His eyes were closed tightly, and his smile was wide and anxious. I can't remember the last time I saw someone so excited. When we finished, he started jumping up and down, just like a little kid, screaming, "I'm saved! I'm saved! Jesus saved me! Yes…yes!"

All around us people were craning their necks to see what the commotion was, but Manny didn't care. He kept jumping up and down, saying, "I'm free! Thank you, Jesus! I'm free!"

That was more than three years ago, and today Manny is busy preparing to be a preacher. With the help of a local church, he went to Bible school and has been studying for a degree in ministry. He never again went back to his life in the streets as a gang member.

Today Manny is on the mountaintop, preparing to go back into the valley where he came from. Back to lead others out of the darkness—to help free other captives from the valley of despair.

PRAYING FOR A BURDEN

If you've spent much of your life on the mountaintop, enjoying the view, trying to forget your days in the valley, don't you think it's time you opened your eyes and looked downward? Down at the people who remain lost and alone, searching for a way out? Down at the ones who need help getting free?

There are so many people like Manny in the world. People who have been through unspeakable pain and sorrow. People who have no father to hold them, to embrace them, to cry with them, to pray with them, to tell them that everything will be all right. To show them the love of Jesus.

When I meet people like Manny, I never feel equipped to take away the pain, but I can do what Jesus would do. I can hold them. Touch them. I can show them what Jesus showed me—that pain is real, but his comfort is even greater. Only he can erase the pain of yesterday. Only God can heal the wounds inflicted by Satan.

Go to your knees today in prayer. And instead of asking God to make your life better, ask him to give you a burden in your heart. A burden for the lost. A burden to help others as God has helped you. Ask him to fill your heart with a soul obsession!

Pray that he will break you out of your life of comfort and security and bring you back to the valley, to someone who was left behind when you started your road up the mountain. And then ask him to help you take her hand as she finds her way free.

Pray for a heart of mercy and compassion. For a mind that is consumed with the same thoughts that consume Jesus. For the strength and wisdom to make a real change in the world—a change that matters.

Jesus came to the valley to help others to freedom. Shouldn't you and I be willing to do the same?

CHAPTER TWELVE

A PASSION FOR COMPASSION

I haven't had a lot of things stolen from me, but several years ago I came home to a real shock. I was casually opening up the mail in my living room when I noticed a credit-card bill. I opened it up, expecting to find a few small charges to our account and instead nearly came out of my shoes. We had over nine thousand dollars charged to our card—in one month!

I immediately started scanning the itemized bill. There was page after page of purchases from places I'd never heard of. Five hundred from one electronics store, eight hundred from another, several large charges from restaurants and grocery stores and clothing outlets—places I'd never been to. I knew in an instant what had happened. Someone had stolen our card.

The first thing I did was to call the credit-card company, and I discovered that a new card had been mailed to us several weeks earlier. The card had obviously been stolen out of our mailbox.

I wasn't prepared for the feelings of anger that came over me. I felt violated, used. *Who would do such a thing? How can they get away with this? Someone has to do something!*

I hung up from the card company and immediately called the police to file a report. They took down all the facts and checked with the neighbors to see if anyone had seen anything. No one had. And without any witnesses, there was little they could do.

I was angry for several days, wondering what I could do to catch the crooks who did this. *They shouldn't get away with it,* I thought as I fumed. *Whoever did this will pay when I catch them.* I even prayed that God would help me find the culprits so that justice could be done.

Then one day, while I was sitting in my living room, once again mulling over this injustice that I had suffered, God convicted my spirit. He reminded me how much I had gotten away with in the past. The many things I had done before coming to Jesus—things that seemed so far back in my past that they no longer felt real to me.

Do you know how much I've forgiven you? God asked in my spirit. *Do you remember what I saved you from? The person who did this is no different than you were the day you gave your life to me. You were just as lost, just as helpless, just as much in need of forgiveness. And I forgave you, just as I want you to forgive the person who did this.*

God put a powerful sense of remorse in my spirit, and I decided at that moment that I would no longer hold any grudge in my heart against the person who stole my credit card. I knew that I needed to let it go and let God decide how to handle it.

It wasn't easy, but from that moment on I made a decision to forgive. It took six months to clear up all the charges to my account, and I was out a lot of time and money when it was all over, but every step of the way I reminded myself to let it go.

Time went by and I was finally able to say that I harbored no more feelings of ill will. I had completely forgiven the person who did it. In fact,

I didn't even think about it much anymore. I thought the matter was over. But that just shows how much God loves to surprise!

SAVED IN COLORADO

Several years later our ministry hosted its first TRUCE outreach to Colorado Springs, my hometown. The crusade drew more people than any of us expected. We had more than 250 workers scouring the city, witnessing in the streets, inviting people to the event. The day of the crusade came, and people packed the stadium. It was one of the largest evangelistic events the city had ever seen. The lines leading to the stadium ran all the way around the building. I had no idea so many people would come. We did two shows a night and still had trouble seating everyone.

Colorado Springs isn't typical of the cities we usually target for outreach. We have more than two hundred ministries based in the city, but that doesn't mean there aren't a lot of people who need Jesus. It didn't feel at first like something God would lead our ministry to do, but his leading was very clear. So we trusted him.

The crowd that showed up that evening was as diverse as it was large. There were white kids, black kids, Latino kids, Asian kids, all kinds of people from all kinds of homes—rich, poor, upper and lower middle class.

During the altar call God's Spirit did a mighty work among us. Hundreds came forward to receive Jesus as their Savior. The newspapers were there in full force, and the next morning our event was on the front page. We were surprised to find that *Inside Edition,* the national news program, sent a team to film the event. They did a special broadcast for their program, and it has been repeated several times since then.

I had no idea what God had planned for our little city. And he wasn't finished yet!

A Simple Note

Several weeks after the crusade, I was sitting in my office when a letter showed up, addressed specifically to me. It had "Personal" written across the bottom, so my secretaries saw that it got right to my hands.

I opened the envelope and took out a small handwritten note. It read, *Dear Mr. Cruz. I'm writing to apologize for something I did several years ago. I stole some mail out of your mailbox, and in it was a credit card...* The letter went on to explain that this man had used my card to buy a lot of extravagant gifts for himself and his friends, and that he only stopped using it after I had the card canceled. He went on to explain that he had been saved the night of our crusade, and that God had now convicted him with guilt over what he had done. *I never would have done this if I'd known who you were,* he wrote. *You've done so much for people through the years, and now that I know Jesus, I know how wrong I've been. I'm now turning my life around, and I want to make things right. Please forgive me. I will repay you any way I can.*

I had planned to write him back, but he had forgotten to include his phone number or address. In a way I was glad, because I would have felt obligated to pursue the matter and turn him in to the credit-card company. I had long since forgiven him, and the credit-card company had already taken care of the debt. His remorse was all God needed from him. I had forgiven him, and now God had forgiven him. I only wish I knew where he was today and what God was doing in his life.

Genuine Mercy

There's nothing that stirs God's heart more than a humble heart and a merciful spirit. God responds to compassion, because it is through compassion that we can fully come to know him. It is the defining quality of a true follower of Christ.

We are never closer to the heart of God than when we are forgiving someone. And we are never farther from it, than when we are holding a grudge. Jesus said, "For if you forgive men when they sin against you, your heavenly Father will also forgive you. But if you do not forgive men their sins, your Father will not forgive your sins" (Matthew 6:14-15). Few scriptures give a clearer insight into what God expects from believers. If you don't forgive, God can't forgive you.

Some years ago I heard the story of two women who had awakened to find a man robbing their home. One of the women was quick thinking enough to call the police, and they were there within a few minutes. Several cars screamed up in front of their house, and the police took the young thief away.

One officer was still at the house, getting all the information he needed from the women and filling out the police report. One of the women asked him what would happen to the young man. "He'll be processed and sent to jail," the policeman told her. "And he probably won't get out for several years."

Even as the officer spoke, the Lord began reminding the woman of a similar incident that had happened some months earlier. Her own son had committed a crime against a family and had been picked up by the police. But at the last minute the family took pity on him and forgave him for his crime. Against the judge's wishes, they refused to press charges, and her son went free.

Then the Lord spoke to her spirit. *I want you to show that same kind of forgiveness,* he told her.

The policeman was busy filling out the forms when she asked him to stop. "Could you do me a favor?" she asked. "Bring the young man back to our house. I want to talk to him before I go any further."

The officer seemed surprised, and he tried to talk her out of it, but the woman persisted. He called the police car on his radio and had the young man brought back to her house. Still in handcuffs, the boy stood before the woman.

"You know what you did was wrong," she told him, "and someone could have gotten hurt. You created a very dangerous situation by trying to rob us, and I just thank God that everyone is all right. But I want you to know that I forgive you for what you've done. I've decided not to press charges. But I want you to remember this and to promise that you'll never do this again."

The man couldn't believe what he was hearing. And the officers weren't too happy with the woman. They tried to convince her to sign the forms and press charges, but she continued to resist. She explained what had happened to her son just six months earlier and told them that the Lord wanted her to forgive.

The boy was released, and he apologized profusely for his crime. He promised the woman that he would never steal again, and she believed him. Before leaving he asked her, "Why are you doing this? I don't deserve your mercy."

"If I don't help you now, who is going to help you change?" she told him.

There is a kind of compassion and mercy that defies human logic. The world doesn't understand it, and it seldom brings much reward. Forgiving others when they do us wrong is one of the most difficult things God can ask us to do. But mercy is what he most wants to see from his followers.

Many might think that this woman was acting more out of stupidity than godly wisdom, and they may very well be right. But if we're going to err, what better way to err than on the side of mercy?

THE COMPASSION OF TRUCE

Of all the things that impress me about the kids who work with us at Nicky Cruz Outreach, our Twelve Disciples, and all the other TRUCE workers who give of their time and talents to help us reach the lost in the inner city, it is their merciful hearts that I most admire. It's the one thing that separates them from most people I know. It's the thing they have in common with one another—what keeps them coming back, day after day, month after month. It's what brings them back to the valley time and time again to reach people for Jesus. Their love is real. Their compassion is deep and genuine. And because of it, their witness is effective.

Before we went to Norway, I remember being concerned about how our kids would react when confronted by hard-core Muslims. Most of them had never run across this type of threat, and I worried for their safety. We spent time talking to them beforehand, preparing them for the anger and verbal abuse they would encounter, but they remained unfazed. Fearless. They didn't even care about their own safety; all they wanted to do was preach Jesus, regardless of the possible consequences.

On the streets of Oslo, I was blown away by how well our workers handled themselves. Many times we were confronted by herds of angry Islamic teenagers, screaming and shouting at us. "Your God is weak," they would say. "Muhammad is stronger than your God." It would have been so easy to get into shouting matches, to defend God against their lies and accusations, to enter into loud arguments, but our kids never once lost focus. They refused to argue. They showed nothing but love and mercy.

"Jesus loves you. And we love you," was their only answer. It was their only response during these brutal confrontations. It continued to catch the Muslim teens and adults off guard and almost always diffused their anger. I never imagined we would see so many Muslims leave their Islamic faith and accept Jesus, but hundreds responded to our message.

I see the same dynamic everywhere we go, whether it's in the inner city of New York, Boston, Hartford, Houston, Milwaukee, St. Louis, Denver, or any other city, whether in this country or abroad. People don't respond to arguments; they respond to compassion. They respond to genuine love and mercy.

Spreading Mercy

And mercy is contagious. While in Norway we teamed with a large Lutheran church in Oslo. It was one of the few churches willing to help us. Their kids were deeply committed to the Lord but caught completely off guard by our methods of evangelism. Europeans are quiet, humble people who usually keep their faith to themselves. The idea of preaching on a street corner, setting up a Hit 'n' Run outreach in the middle of a neighborhood, took them far from their comfort zones. At first they didn't want to go with us, but within a few weeks we couldn't stop them. They developed a fire in their guts for evangelism—a genuine soul obsession.

Many of them traveled by train for two or three hours each morning to help us, then traveled home again late in the evening. They couldn't get enough. And they were so thirsty to learn more about our kids from New York. When we told them that many of our kids were former gang members and drug addicts, they had a hard time believing it. They were astonished by what Jesus had done in their lives—what he was still doing.

But what attracted them most was the genuine compassion our kids had for others. When someone was hurting, our kids would cry with them, hold them, pray with them. Every morning began with several hours of prayer and worship at the church building, and the Lutheran kids couldn't get enough of it. The love our kids exuded for them and one another was beyond anything they had ever experienced. And they soon caught that enthusiasm. It spread like a wildfire throughout the hearts of everyone working with us.

By the time our crusade ended, the kids from Norway couldn't bear to see us leave. They had become so attached to our group, so in love with our kids, that they cried for hours at the airport before our plane left. Our kids made lifetime friends on that trip and made an indelible impact on the lives of those we left behind—an impact that is still being felt in corners of Oslo.

That's the beauty and nature of compassion. It is one of the most endearing and contagious of all human emotions. It can't be faked, and its impact can't be explained, yet it is so real. And so very powerful.

No Time for Religion

There is a time and place for arguing doctrine and debating theology, but not when trying to reach someone for Christ. One of the greatest strengths of our ministry is that we decided years ago to leave theology to the scholars and instead focus only on the love of Jesus. When we reach out to a neighborhood, we leave our arguments at home and bring only a soft shoulder and a tender heart. We love people because Jesus has put a burden in our hearts to save them. And the more we reach out, the greater our compassion grows.

So often on the streets someone will walk up to me with fire in his eyes, wanting to get into a religious debate. Often we get people from a Mormon church, or a Jehovah's Witness, or even an Islamic extremist, and they want to argue about our beliefs or our methods. I never allow myself to be drawn in. I tell them, "Let someone else take you to Harvard University. The only school I'm interested in is the University of the Holy Spirit."

I'm sure that there are a few people on earth who have been saved through theological debate, but I've never met one. It's the love of Jesus that people respond to. I tell them about the Cross, about the forgiveness that Jesus brings, and then pray for a miracle in their hearts, and that's what drives them to their knees in repentance. That's what brings them before the throne of Jesus.

God works a miracle in their hearts, because a miracle is what they most need.

Seeds of Forgiveness

I wish you could experience the miracle that our family has experienced. I wish you could feel the difference between how we live now and how we lived during the days of my youth. Today I love my brothers and sister with a passion. There's nothing I'd rather do than to sit around and laugh and talk and cry with my family.

The times that I get to travel back to Puerto Rico and visit are some of my most precious memories. When I go home I'm no longer Nicky Cruz the evangelist or speaker; I'm just a brother. To my older brothers I am "little Nicky." To my younger ones I am "big Nicky." But none of them see me as "big shot Nicky!" I'm just one of the family, and I love that. In fact two of my brothers pastor churches in Puerto Rico, and they've never even asked me to speak to their congregations. They know that when I come home I come to play and hang out.

I have so many memories of staying up late with my family, eating and laughing and joking and praying and crying together. Sometimes we stay up until one o'clock in the morning telling stories. Trading jokes. Enjoying the joy we all share. It's like one big fiesta!

But that's not how it used to be with us. We weren't always so happy and carefree and loving. When Jesus came into our lives, he brought with him an explosion of love! He opened the floodgates of mercy and forgiveness. In my family we have a lot of pain in our past, yet none of us harbors feelings of resentment. No one holds a grudge. We hold nothing but love in our hearts among us. We don't spend any time in regret; we just rejoice in the Jesus we know today—in the future he brings to us all.

It breaks my heart to see families that hold on to the past. Brothers and sisters who hang on to bitterness and resentment from days long gone. Husbands and wives who have been hurt by words or actions, so they allow the pain to fester, to grow, to eat away at them like a cancer. They hold grudges in their hearts and never learn to forgive. Never learn the joy of looking forward. The joy of laughing and playing together with those they are supposed to love. The peace of putting old hurts to rest and allowing Jesus to heal the wounds.

Jesus can do for the human heart what no one else can do. He can bring about change unlike anything we could imagine. When he comes to live in your heart, he does more than forgive you, he leaves behind seeds of forgiveness. Supernatural seeds that will not only erase the sin, but erase the pain that sin has brought. Not only can these seeds heal our hearts, they can heal our relationships as well. They can heal the wounds inflicted upon others. They can spread through every hurt of our past and undo it.

Jesus can bring families together again. Mothers and fathers and brothers and sisters. Friends and enemies, old and new. He can bridge any gap we've created. Restore any home we've wrecked. Rebuild any heart we've broken.

I could never thank Jesus enough for what he has done for our family. For the forgiveness and mercy and grace that he brought, bringing us back together again.

And he can do the same for anyone. For any family. Even yours, if that's what you need!

Abram fell facedown, and God said to him, "As for me, this is my covenant with you: You will be the father of many nations. No longer will you be called Abram; your name will be Abraham."

GENESIS 17:3-5

Come now, let's make a covenant, you and I, and let it serve as a witness between us.

GENESIS 31:44

But I have raised you up for this very purpose.

EXODUS 9:16

Now if you obey me fully and keep my covenant, then out of all nations you will be my treasured possession. Although the whole earth is mine, you will be for me a kingdom of priests and a holy nation.

EXODUS 19:5-6

After the supper he took the cup, saying, "This cup is the new covenant in my blood, which is poured out for you."

LUKE 22:20

He has made us competent as ministers of a new covenant—not of the letter but of the Spirit; for the letter kills, but the Spirit gives life.

2 CORINTHIANS 3:6

CHAPTER THIRTEEN

A NEW FUTURE

W hen I first made my commitment to God, I had nothing to give him but my heart. I was a cocky and socially unskilled gangster. A kid from the streets.

I went to a Bible college in California to straighten my life out, to get away from New York and the gang life, but I quickly discovered that I didn't fit in there. I may have been saved, but I was still a confused boy. I still strutted around with my long hair and jitterbug walk, and people were turned off by it. I wanted to change, but I didn't know how.

It was a lonely time of my life. I made friends, but they weren't like the friends I had in New York. I had nothing in common with them. They didn't understand me, and I didn't understand them. Most nights I just stayed in my small dorm room, wondering what I was going to do with the rest of my life.

Though I was in Bible college, I never had an interest in becoming a preacher or an evangelist. With my thick Latino accent, I couldn't imagine God calling me to do such a thing. I couldn't imagine him using me for *anything.* What good was I? What good could I do for God? I was so confused and lost.

So many nights I prayed to God for some kind of direction. "Please show me what to do next," I would plead. But I never felt an answer.

Longing for a Future

One night I was in my room feeling more lost and alone than ever. I was broken and completely spent—no emotional energy left.

I was lying on the floor, flat on my back, staring up at the ceiling. The room was dark, except for a few rays of light beaming across the walls from the streetlights outside the window. I traced the rays from one corner of the room to the other with my eyes.

My heart was completely empty. I felt nothing but loneliness. My spirit was completely broken. I remember thinking back to my days on the streets of New York, before giving my life to Jesus. I had done so many things that haunted me. The guilt I felt in my heart was overwhelming, and it wouldn't let me go. Over and over I had prayed for God to take away the guilt and pain, but he didn't. I couldn't get away from it.

While lying on the floor, I began to pray again. "God, why do I have to suffer so much? What do you want me to do? I'm so lost and you're so silent. I love you, God. You know how much I love you. But I don't know what you want from me! Please give me a sense of direction and peace. Please show me what you want!"

For four hours I lay on the floor pleading with God to break his silence. The more time went by, the more numbness I felt in my spirit. The room grew darker, and my heart grew weaker.

Then suddenly I felt an amazing calm in my spirit. It came over me like a wave. I closed my eyes and took a deep breath. I could feel God speaking into my heart. I could sense his presence. *Nicky,* he said to my spirit, *my son, don't worry. I haven't forgotten you. I brought you to this place for a purpose. I've separated you from your friends and your past, and now I'm giving you a new future. I have plans for you, Nicky. I need you to trust me. I'm going to raise you up as an evangelist. I'm going to use you to touch the lives of young people. But you need to have faith. I'll never leave you. I'll always be right here by your side.*

For the longest time I lay on the floor, basking in God's presence as he calmed my spirit. I couldn't imagine that I was hearing him right. *How could I possibly become an evangelist? I've got so much baggage from my past. I've got nothing to give—nothing but my testimony. Why would God choose someone like me?*

I told God how much I loved him and how much I wanted to serve him. I asked him if he wanted me to go back to New York and confess to the police about all the things I had done. "I'm willing to pay the consequences for my past if that's what you want from me," I told him. "Just let me know what you want me to do, and I'll do it."

But the more I talked, the more I sensed him saying, *Just trust me, Nicky. Stay faithful and I'll show you what I want you to do. I'm going to raise you up as an evangelist. But you need to have faith. You need to listen and follow when I lead.*

A Covenant to Embrace

God has been faithful to that covenant for more than forty years. Though I wasn't capable of comprehending his plans for me at the time, he remained true. As the months and years went by, I continued to feel his direction. With each passing day he confirmed this covenant even more. Through good and bad times he has always been there, always watched over me.

When God gives a gift, he never takes it back. He never goes back on his promises.

Many times over the years I have veered from my purpose. I've doubted God and strayed from his plan for my life. But he has always brought me back. He continued to remind me of this covenant he had made for me—this life vision that I didn't understand or ask for. But it has brought me more joy and reward than I could possibly deserve.

God didn't make this covenant *with* me; he made it *for* me. It was his idea, not mine. I couldn't even comprehend such a thing for my life, but God could.

So often I see people trying to make covenants with God. They decide in their hearts what they want God to do for them and begin praying for it. They set a plan in motion and then ask God to bless it. They claim scriptures for themselves, then remind God that he is supposed to be faithful in helping them carry out the plan. But they've missed the point. God doesn't work that way. He doesn't wait for us to come up with a plan—he already has one. What he wants is people who will accept the future that he has already prepared for them.

JUST A SHEPHERD BOY

David was just a young shepherd boy, tending his father's sheep, when God picked him to become the king of Israel. God had rejected Saul as king because of his wickedness and instead sent his prophet Samuel to seek out David—a mere shepherd boy. "[David] was ruddy, with a fine appearance and handsome features. Then the LORD said, 'Rise and anoint him; he is the one.' So Samuel took the horn of oil and anointed him in the presence of his brothers, and from that day on the Spirit of the LORD came upon David in power" (1 Samuel 16:12-13).

Try to imagine what David must have felt at the time. How could he possibly have imagined becoming king of Israel? Did he even comprehend what was going on? He was just a boy tending sheep, probably grooming himself to take over his father's business someday. The job of shepherd was the lowliest job a person could have. As the youngest son of Jesse, David was sent to the fields each day to tend to the flocks; his brothers handled the "more important" jobs. Even his own father couldn't see the greatness inside of David's heart. He was destined to live and die as a common sheepherder.

But God changed all of that. God saw David's heart and stepped in to create a covenant for him—a grand and glorious future far better than David could have dreamed for himself.

At the time David was content just spending time in the fields alone with God. He would run through the grass and sing before the Lord, worshiping and praying and taking in the beautiful mountain air. Early in the morning he would find a spot on a tall rock and watch the majestic sunrise, breathing in the colors as they changed from moment to moment. Each morning he suckled on the northern wind, strengthening his bones by drinking in the freedom of the open space.

It was here in the fields that David first connected with God. That he learned to talk to him as a friend. That's why the psalms of David are so beautiful and inspiring. In the psalms he takes us back to the days when it was just him and God, dancing in the fields together, tending to the sheep, growing in love and friendship.

"The heavens declare the glory of God; the skies proclaim the work of his hands. Day after day they pour forth speech; night after night they display knowledge…. In the heavens he has pitched a tent for the sun, which is like a bridegroom coming forth from his pavilion, like a champion rejoicing to run his course. It rises at one end of the heavens and makes its circuit to the other; nothing is hidden from its heat" (Psalm 19:1-2,4-6).

As a shepherd David loved God with a passion. And God took notice.

A Covenant for You

Are you waiting on a covenant from God, on a vision, on a purpose for your future? Are you longing to do great things for God—to serve him and love him until your dying breath? Are you wanting God to define a glorious future for you?

Then stop trying to do it on your own. Don't try to set a course for your life and then ask God to bless it. Instead spend your time getting to know him. Learn to bask in his presence. To worship him with abandon. To praise him and love him from the depths of your soul. To obey him, even in the smallest detail. To pray and meditate on his Word. To appreciate the glory of creation.

Learn to set your heart on God, and God alone, and he will take notice.

There is one truth you can know for certain: God has a covenant prepared just for you. A special plan and purpose set aside for your future. And it is more glorious than you could ever imagine on your own. If he hasn't laid this covenant on your heart, it is only because he knows you are not ready. He's waiting on you. Watching. Longing to share this vision with you and help you embrace it.

And the saddest part is that many live and die having never received nor accepted this glorious future that God had in store for them.

When I was a young man in my early twenties, lying on the floor of my dorm room, confused about my future, I could never have imagined the plans God had for my life. I was just a young boy in love with Jesus, longing to spend the rest of my days in his presence. I had no idea he had a covenant prepared for me. No idea he had such a powerful purpose in store for my life.

I could have easily missed it and gone another direction. When God laid his plans on my heart, I could have rejected his covenant and gone my own way. I could have convinced myself that I hadn't heard him right, or decided that I had other ideas for my career, and forfeited the life God had in store for me.

At the time I couldn't even begin to imagine myself as an evangelist. I was young and unprepared. I had no capabilities that would have led me to think that I could preach in front of an audience. My Bible knowledge was immature and limited. My accent was thick. My manners were awkward. I was just a streetwise kid, and that was all I had going for me.

But I loved Jesus with a passion, and I determined to obey God, regardless of what he would have me do. So I embraced his covenant, little by little, day by day, month by month. I tried my best to stay faithful. And God has never let me down.

I still remember the first few times I was asked to give my testimony before a crowd. The idea scared me to death, and everything within me wanted to run and hide—to just get a job somewhere and live a peaceful life. But I knew that God was grooming me, preparing me, pushing me to greater things. So I obeyed God and even made a fool of myself several times. I accepted the future he had in store for me. And because of it, I've been able to live a life of joy and fulfillment that I never imagined possible.

I'm still that little boy in the dormitory, staring at the ceiling, wondering what God has in store for me. I still marvel at the plans he has for my future. I still wonder where he will take me next, what he will have me do. I'm not as confused as I used to be, but I'm still incapable of comprehending the great things he has in store. Every day he surprises me with new and exciting possibilities.

My life is defined by a series of covenants with God, each one playing a small role in this larger vision for my life that he set in motion more than forty years ago. He has made countless promises to me through the years and has never once failed to fulfill them. He has never been unfaithful, even though my faithfulness has often fallen short.

Though I never intentionally disobey God, I have often taken wrong detours. So many times I moved away from God, tried to do things on my own, but he always brought me back. Always stayed with me. He continued to groom and disciple me, helping me fulfill the purpose that he set aside for my future.

I still take detours from time to time, and I probably will until the day I die, but I know that God will never let me down. Like David, I plan to spend the rest of my days serving him, loving him, following him. And with the last breath in my lungs I will sing, "For great is your love, reaching to the heavens; your faithfulness reaches to the skies" (Psalm 57:10).

CHAPTER FOURTEEN

WRONG DETOURS

My first job in ministry was with Teen Challenge in New York. After Bible college God brought me back to minister in the streets where I once ran aimlessly, terrorizing anyone who crossed my path. The streets where my gang still lived.

David Wilkerson founded Teen Challenge as an outreach to the streets of New York, and then he asked me to be the first director. I had no idea why God had called me back to the city, but I trusted him and went.

It was during my time there that a publisher approached me to write my first book. David Wilkerson's book about my conversion, *The Cross and the Switchblade,* had become an international bestseller, putting my name and story in the limelight. So a publisher approached me to write my own story. At first I had a catch in my spirit and didn't want to do it. I turned him down the first time he called, but the publisher persisted. He talked about the money we would make and the possibilities for a movie in the future, and I was running out of reasons to resist. So I told him to send over a contract and I would sign it.

Throughout the process I continued to feel uneasy about it. I wasn't sure why, and I prayed for God to give me a sense of peace. It never came. I continued to pray, and the publisher continued to tell me how excited they were about the book. So I chalked up my uneasiness to nerves and moved forward with the project. I had already signed a contract and couldn't imagine that God would want me to go back on my word.

One day I was talking to Gloria and I asked her, "How do you feel about me telling my story?"

Gloria thought for a moment and said, "If this is what God wants you to do, you should do it. It's your story, and only you can answer that question. If God wants to use your past for his glory, you should let them print your story. I know your past is a brutal one, but our kids will understand. God will work it out."

Even though I continued to feel uneasy, I moved forward with the book. We still didn't have a title for it, and the publisher was pressing me to come up with a good one. I prayed about it, but nothing came. Then one day I saw my little baby, Alicia, running through the kitchen, laughing. She looked so cute with her diaper hanging down on her hips. I laughed aloud and said without thinking, "Run, baby, run."

At that moment I realized that I had a title for my book. *Run Baby Run*. It perfectly described the life I had lived before coming to Jesus. I called the publisher, and he was as excited about it as I was. We finally had a title.

Run Baby Run was published in 1968, and it immediately became a bestseller. No one was prepared for the success of this simple book written by an unknown kid from the ghetto and printed by a relatively small publisher. It started out as a bestseller, then rose to the status of "publishing phenomenon," and today, more than thirty-five years later, I often hear it referred to as a "Christian classic." The book is still in print in more than forty countries and continues to be a bestseller.

How could I have imagined what God had planned for this simple book? How could I have comprehended the way God would use my story to touch lives throughout the world? I still don't understand why he chose to do so.

And yet I've never forgotten the catch I had in my spirit while it was being written. Why did I continue to feel so uneasy? Why did God seem so silent when I prayed for guidance? What was he trying to tell me?

Missing God's Purpose

Today I am convinced that although God wanted my story to be told, he was trying to lead me to a different publisher. The nervousness I felt was God's warning in my spirit. He was trying to get my attention. But in my immaturity, I didn't see it.

In my last book, *One Holy Fire,* I revealed for the first time the numerous problems I dealt with through the publication of my first book. I didn't do this to open old wounds but to simply show how God can work through our failures and use them for good. Although *Run Baby Run* was a worldwide bestseller, I was receiving almost no money for it. The publisher always seemed to have an excuse for this, but it now seems obvious that I was being taken advantage of. And I had no idea how to combat the problem. I still don't know all of the dynamics involved, only that God used the book for his glory—and continues to use it—in spite of the publisher's wrong intentions or motives.

But God tried to warn me. He attempted to get my attention and lead me elsewhere—maybe to a larger, more established publisher. I'm certain

God's blessing was on my book, but he had other plans for how it was supposed to be published. And had I paid attention, or been able to recognize his warnings, I would have saved myself endless headaches through the years.

It was just one example of how God has taught me to listen when he tries to speak into my heart. So often I sense God guiding me, directing me down a different path, showing me his will. And through many instances like this one, I've learned little by little how to recognize his gentle nudges.

A DIFFERENT PATH

This isn't the only detour I've taken from the many paths God has set before me in my life. I've spent a lot of time going in the wrong direction, but God always seems to bring me back. God has never forgotten the covenant that he made with me those many years ago in my dorm room in California, and no matter how often I stray from my calling, he remains faithful.

Early in my ministry I developed a love for working with teens, and I've often wanted to be able to work more closely with them on a day-to-day basis. As an evangelist I don't always get to do that. I speak to large crowds and then minister to those who come forward for prayer, but it isn't the same. Often I leave the next day and never see them again.

My years as director of Teen Challenge in New York taught me how fulfilling it can be to work with kids in a center. At Teen Challenge we ministered to recovering drug addicts, teen alcoholics, and kids from broken and abusive homes. We dealt with runaways and prostitutes and gang members—kids who had been through hell in their short lives. I was able to live among them and embrace their pain as it came. Throughout the center we had cots and mattresses on the floor, and they would be filled with drug addicts going through withdrawal or ex-gangsters and prostitutes looking for a place to rest and hide from harm.

So many times during the night I would hear their cries and make my way downstairs to find them reeling in pain or shaking from a bad nightmare. I would cover them with warm blankets and hold wet cloths on their foreheads until they could get back to sleep. Though I was young, I was like a father to them—the only father many of them ever had. I would talk to them, embrace them, feed them, help them any way I could. If they threw up on the floor, I would dig out a handful of rags and clean up the mess. If they needed to make a call, I would dial the phone for them. If they needed to cry, I would be there to cry with them. It was one of the most emotionally draining times of my life. And it was by far the most rewarding.

A Center in Raleigh

Because of that experience, I dreamed of building teen centers throughout the country. I longed to spend my days running one of the centers, perhaps living nearby and having my family help with the daily chores. I was sure God would bless such a venture, since he was the one who placed a burden for teens in my heart.

Through the years we have started more than seventeen centers in different cities, and always God blessed our efforts. But I never allowed myself the freedom to direct the centers that we opened. Once they were up and running, I would turn them over to capable hands and continue my work as an evangelist. But somewhere in my heart I always longed to settle down

171

and spend my days working with teens in one of our centers. I often wondered if God would let me.

During one period of my life, years ago, I moved my family to Raleigh, North Carolina, to open up a center for girls. In my mind it was going to be an extension of my ministry. I would still be an evangelist and travel as God led me, but my free time would be spent running the center. Gloria continued to remind me that this wasn't what God called me to do, but I didn't listen.

It was an amazingly rewarding venture. I still remember the day we were dedicating the center. Gloria was pregnant with our fourth daughter, Elena, at the time. She had never been so sick during a pregnancy.

Elena was conceived in South Africa, and I've often teased her about it. "That's why you have such a strange accent," I tell her.

Gloria is a strong woman, and she can take a lot of pain, but this pregnancy was really taking its toll. She couldn't sleep, her feet were swollen, and it was often all she could do to get around. There was nothing I could do to help except try to keep her off her feet—which wasn't easy with Gloria.

One of Gloria's best friends in Raleigh was Anne Graham Lotz, the daughter of Billy Graham. Anne was an enormous help to Gloria during her pregnancy. I felt guilty because I was traveling so much and working all my spare time to get the center ready to open, so it was nice to know that Gloria had Anne by her side.

By the time the center was ready to be dedicated, Gloria was just a few weeks from delivering. She was in terrible pain during the whole pregnancy. The center was a beautiful building, finely decorated, like a small mansion. And many notables came to see it open. Anne was there, along with Senator Jesse Helms and a number of other congressmen and celebrities. The news reporters showed up to record the event. I felt terrible that

Gloria was in so much pain and discomfort. She couldn't enjoy the dedication, even though she had done so much work to help get the center ready to open.

During the ceremony, Gloria noticed a young girl hanging around the front porch, so she went to talk with her. He name was Mary, and she had no place to go. She had heard about our center for girls and came to see if it was open yet. Gloria took her by the hand and led her through the halls and into one of the back rooms. There the two of them sat and talked throughout much of the ceremony.

At one point I wondered where Gloria had gone and found her in the back room with this young girl. Gloria was witnessing to her and crying with her. She had completely forgotten her pain and almost forgotten that there was a ceremony going on in the main hall. That evening Gloria led Mary to Christ, and she became our first convert in the new center.

What better way to dedicate a teen center in God's honor than to lead someone to salvation in the midst of it? The house may have been filled with important and highbrow people, but the event God cared about most was the one going on in the back room.

More than any story I can think of, this one defines what kind of person Gloria is. She loves people with a passion and has a heart the size of Texas. She has a true soul obsession. I've never met anyone as real and genuine and caring as Gloria. And we've long since lost count of how many people she's brought to Christ. That's why I love her so much.

BETTER OR BEST?

Our teen center in Raleigh became a tremendous success through the years. We ministered to hundreds of teens and brought most of them to Christ. It was clear that God's blessing was on us. But the more our center grew, the less time I had for evangelism. I still traveled all I could, but often I would have to decline invitations to speak at an evangelistic crusade or event.

I wasn't too bothered about this at first, since I would rather be home at the center. But little by little it began to bother me more. Somehow it didn't feel right. I loved overseeing the center and working alongside Gloria to minister to the young girls who came for help, but I knew in my heart that God had called me for a different purpose. And Gloria knew it too.

One day she came to me in frustration and said, "Nicky, I know you love these kids. I know you love doing this. I do too. But is this what God wants you doing? You've always said God called you to be an evangelist, but now you're spending more time at the center than you are speaking. Have you been praying about this? Has God changed your calling?"

I know it was a difficult thing for Gloria to say to me, since she loved the center so much. And she loved the time that I was able to spend at home with her and the girls. But something in her spirit told her that she needed to confront me, so she obeyed.

In many ways I had been feeling the same thing. I've always been sensitive to God's leading, and I promised him early in my ministry that I would never turn down an opportunity to evangelize when he brought it my way, yet now I found myself looking for excuses to stay home. In my spirit I knew what God wanted me to do, yet I struggled to follow through.

In my heart of hearts, I knew that Gloria was right. As much as I loved running the center, and as much good as we were doing, I had detoured from my true calling. It was good work, but it wasn't what God set me aside to do.

I spent a lot of time praying and meditating over the next few months, seeking God's guidance. And the more I did, the clearer it became. God made a covenant with me. He made me an evangelist. And he had always blessed me when I stayed true to that purpose. It was time to get back on track and once again embrace my covenant.

As I continued to seek God, I sensed him telling me to turn the center over to some capable people and move my family to Colorado Springs, Colorado. It was a strange request, since we didn't know anyone in Colorado, but God wouldn't let me rest until I did. Gloria was terribly sad when I told her about it, since she had so many good friends in North Carolina, but she knew that we needed to obey.

Leaving our friends in Raleigh was one of the most difficult things we've ever done. And at the time we had no idea why God called us away. But now, years later, we can see what God had in store for us. Had we not moved, TRUCE ministries may never have been born. And we would never have met Jim and Mary Irwin—two people who have made an indelible impact on our lives.

God's Perfect Will

So how does God feel about it when we take detours from the path he has set us on? Does God really care when we veer from a good work as long as we venture into another work that is equally noble and virtuous? Why would God care if I ministered to kids in a teen center or testified in front of a filled stadium? Both tasks lead people to Jesus. Both are expanding the kingdom. And both are things that are near to God's heart. Is it really that important to God how we serve him as long as we serve him?

Many might argue with me on this point, but I'm convinced that God has a specific role set aside for each of us. He has given us unique gifts and talents and desires, and he has created an individual covenant for us that fits those gifts. "For I know the plans I have for you," God told us through his prophet Jeremiah (29:11). Nothing is left to chance when it comes to God. Long before he created us he knew what he wanted us to accomplish. He knew the people that he wanted us to touch and that he wanted to put into our lives in order to touch us. You and I were created for a purpose, and God's perfect plan is for us to embrace that purpose.

God can use our detours for good, but he longs for us to stay the course. Because what he has in store is so much better than what we could possibly find on our own. I know a man who used to pastor a large church in Brooklyn. He had a powerful and thriving ministry to the poor. I worked with him several times, and it was easy to see how well suited he was for this church. People flocked to hear him speak, and the congregation was thriving.

But he came under pressure from some of the more wealthy members to move his church to Staten Island, to a more respectable, middle-class neighborhood. The pastor resisted for some time, but soon the pressure began to mount. The members continued to lobby for a move and even started looking for a place to relocate.

The pastor finally relented. The church sold its building and moved the congregation to an upscale building in Staten Island. Many poor people couldn't make the drive, and they had to find other churches to attend. The pastor continued to preach strong sermons, but it was clear that his heart was in Brooklyn. He had detoured from the calling that God had for him.

His new church thrived and continued to grow and prosper, but those of us who know this pastor and his heart know that he should have stayed in Brooklyn. God has blessed his new ministry, but many people were hurt through the ordeal. He's still a powerful pastor with a thriving ministry, but I'm convinced that God had—and still has—other plans for him.

So what blessings has this pastor forfeited by veering from God's covenantal plan for his life? He may never know.

And what blessings did I forfeit during the years that I veered from God's covenantal plan for my life? I may never know. At least not until I get to heaven!

FOLLOWING THE RIGHT PATH

We all take detours from God's plan, and we will do so until the day we die. God is patient and faithful just the same. But how much better would our lives be if we strived every day to stay the course that God sets before us? How many people could we bless if we allowed God to work through us each day? How much more effective would we be in life and ministry if we only learned to let God set our agenda?

I'm still not sure why God chose to take me as a young Christian and mold me into an evangelist. Every day I see preachers who are much more polished and articulate than I am. I wonder why God didn't have them speaking to the large crowds instead of me. He could have easily used me to run teen centers or pastor a church or work in some other line of ministry. But this is the covenant that he made for me, and so I carry it out the best I know how.

And what about you? Have you embraced the covenant that God has prepared for you? Have you sought out his purpose for your life and then set yourself toward fulfilling it? Or are you living your life by taking one detour after another?

It's a question that each one of us needs to ask. And one that God is waiting to answer.

CHAPTER FIFTEEN

BLINDED BY SIN

Not all detours are innocent ones. Sometimes our detours take us down roads of sin and disobedience—places far away from God and his plan for our lives.

I know many pastors who have had thriving ministries before getting caught up in sin and corruption. Some have fallen to adultery or other sexual sins. Others have sinned through acts of greed or disobedience. Still others have simply failed to live up to their calling before God.

One particular evangelist had a powerful anointing on his ministry. Wherever he spoke he packed stadiums, and thousands were coming to Christ through his testimony. His ministry was touching lives all over the world, and God was using him mightily. Until he got involved with another woman. He tried to hide his affair, and for a time it worked. But then he got caught, and the public scandal ruined him. He eventually left his mistress and tried to rebuild his marriage, but the damage had already been done. His ministry was brought down, and his influence dwindled to nothing.

Today he's trying to put his life back together. He's speaking again, trying to rebuild the ministry that he lost, but it will never be what it was. The credibility he lost will never be regained.

Proverbs 6:32-33 tells us, "But a man who commits adultery lacks judgment; whoever does so destroys himself. Blows and disgrace are his lot, and his shame will never be wiped away."

Many ministers have learned this lesson only after it was too late.

A MAN AFTER GOD'S HEART

No one knows the damage that sin can do better than King David.

Who lived more in the blessing of God than King David? As king of Israel he had everything a man could possibly want—every privilege a man can imagine. He lived and dined in the finest palace in the world and was surrounded by servants and friends and women who adored him. He was wealthy beyond imagination. His palace was filled with gold and precious jewels and fine linen—riches beyond compare.

As the leader of Israel's vast army he was a fearless warrior, a powerful general. Nothing intimidated him. Enemies trembled at the sight of him. Friends bowed as he passed. Women swooned at his power and presence. He knew he was moving under the protection of God, and he feared no man. There was no army that could stand in his way—no soldier that could survive a confrontation with David's sword.

Even as a boy David knew the power and protection of God. Grown men cowered at the sight of Goliath, the giant, but not David. He took him on with nothing but a slingshot in his hand and brought the giant down. He faced lions with bare hands and bears with nothing but a spear. God took a small, insignificant country boy, a shepherd, and turned him into a mighty warrior-king!

No ruler had the kind of love and respect that David enjoyed. The people adored him, his servants obeyed him without question, his wives fulfilled his every need and desire. What man has ever lived in such blessing? such favor? such grace and approval from the Creator?

Yet all of that paled in comparison to his relationship with God. He loved God with a passion and worshiped him with abandon. Even in the midst of his many duties, David spent hour after hour writing songs and poems to God, singing to God from his heart, courting the Creator of the universe as one lover courts another. All the gold and silver and riches in the world meant nothing to David compared to his relationship with God. That was the secret to his power. That was what made David such an awesome ruler and king.

He knew without any reservation that he could do nothing without God. He knew this from the time he was a small shepherd boy, tending his father's sheep. Even then David depended on God for his every breath, for his every waking moment. David knew that God provided the strength in his bones, the blood in his veins, the wisdom in his mind, and the courage in his heart. And he never questioned this truth.

"It is God who arms me with strength," wrote David, "and makes my way perfect. He makes my feet like the feet of a deer; he enables me to stand on the heights. He trains my hands for battle; my arms can bend a bow of bronze. You give me your shield of victory; you stoop down to make me great. You broaden the path beneath me, so that my ankles do not turn. I pursued my enemies and crushed them; I did not turn back till they were destroyed. I crushed them completely, and they could not rise; they fell beneath my feet. You armed me with strength for battle; you made my adversaries bow at my feet" (2 Samuel 22:33-40).

The greatest king and warrior who ever lived knew exactly what made him great. He knew that he was nothing without his Lord and Savior. But even David's unmatched, unquenchable, unmistakable love for God didn't stop him from noticing a pretty woman.

BLINDED BY BEAUTY

How beautiful must Bathsheba have been to turn the head of King David? What kind of woman would it take to distract a man so completely and wholly in love with God?

David had thousands of women to choose from—both wives and concubines. Surely there were dozens of utterly striking women among them. Women who would willingly give themselves to him at any moment. Women who were legally and morally free to do so. But one glance at Bathsheba, and David forgot every one of them. One glance at this spectacular beauty on the roof next door, and David lost all sense of right and wrong. One glance from Bathsheba did what Goliath was incapable of doing—what thousands of warriors and fierce animals couldn't do. It brought David to his knees.

For one night in the arms of Bathsheba, David was willing to turn his back on everything he knew to be right and just and moral. He was willing to compromise everything God had ever done for him, every blessing God had given him, every principle he had held so dear, every soldier that had ever died for him, every woman who had ever loved him.

David was willing to disgrace the God who made him what he was, who gave him everything he ever had, for a single moment of passion in the arms of Bathsheba.

If you don't think Satan knows how to bring a man down, then you don't know anything about Satan. At the moment of our greatest strength, he knows how to find our one weakness. And he knows exactly how to target that chink in our armor.

Bathsheba was the one woman in all of Israel beautiful enough to bring David down, and Satan moved her right next door to the palace. He is a cold and cunning enemy, and no man should ever take him for granted. No man should ever believe that he is invincible against sin.

THE PRICE OF SIN

David paid a high price for his rendezvous with Bathsheba. His hands would be forever stained with Uriah's blood, and his illegitimate child would be taken from him. He disgraced himself in front of his friends and servants. And worst of all, he compromised his relationship with God. "Out of your own household I am going to bring calamity upon you," the Lord told David. "Before your very eyes I will take your wives and give them to one who is close to you, and he will lie with your wives in broad daylight. You did it in secret, but I will do this thing in broad daylight, before all Israel" (2 Samuel 12:11-12).

On top of all this, David lost the privilege of building God's temple. The task would be handed down to his son Solomon. Can we even imagine what David must have been thinking? what he must have been going through? how much he must have agonized over his sin with Bathsheba?

David had lived his entire life in the favor and grace of God. There was nothing he longed for more than God's approval. Nothing that meant more to him than feeling God near. Resting in his presence. Dancing with his Lord and Savior.

How cold and barren his palace must have felt. How empty the gold and silver and granite riches surrounding him must have seemed. I can see him sitting in a cold, dark corner of his exquisite bedroom, his knees under his chin and his cheeks streaked with tears of sorrow, crying out to God, pleading for God to come near, to forgive him, to once again draw him into his presence. "Don't take your Spirit away from me," he cried out in agony. "I am nothing without my Maker, my Savior, my Lover!" (see Psalm 51:11).

Did his mind drift back to the days of his childhood—his days of tending sheep in the fields? He imagined himself once again singing and dancing with God, praising him from morning to night, basking in his presence, laughing as they walked and talked together. He saw himself smiling as God touched his cheek, brushed his hair, kissed his heart. He pictured himself leaning against a rock as his sheep grazed in the fields before him, writing a love note to God, line after line of precious words of adoration. Page after page of praise. Song after song of eloquent psalms, expressing his undying affection for his Lord and Savior.

He saw himself as a boy sitting on the floor of his cold, dank home in the fields. The northern wind bit his skin as it blew through the window of his humble quarters. He pulled his blanket tighter to fend off the breeze. He was so happy then, so poor, but so in love with God. So sure of God's grace on his life. So content with the small blessings his Lord had provided. Day after day he sat meditating on God's glory, imagining his face, feeling his Lord's favor.

He longed to go back to those days, back to the days of simplicity and grace and innocence. The days before he found himself burdened with the responsibilities of being a king and a warrior. Before he had to deal with finances, construction, administration, transportation, military maneuvers, wives, children, subjects, soldiers, wars, and all the other trappings of being a mighty king! *Why is life so hard now?* he thought. *So complicated? So burdening? Why can't it be like it was before? I don't want all the riches and respon-*

sibilities! I don't want a palace! I don't want to be a ruler! I just want my Lord, my God, my Lover!

David's sin cost him the one thing he could never live without. The one thing he most treasured, most needed, most longed to have. It cost him God's nearness!

Hard as he tried, he couldn't feel God's presence anymore. He couldn't connect with his heart. And the pain was more than he could bear.

A HEART LONGING FOR GOD

That's why God loved David with such passion. This is the heart that God saw when he looked into David's chest. This is what brought David into such favor with his Lord.

Even on the heels of his greatest sin, his thoughts were consumed with visions of God, with longings for God's nearness and grace. He didn't care what his sin would cost him as long as he could once again feel God's favor. No physical consequence mattered. He would pay any price to once again feel God's approval, sense his smile, experience his loving embrace.

Can you relate to David? Have you ever found yourself far from God, longing to once again be back in his arms? back in his blessing? back in his loving embrace?

There are times in my life when things get so complicated and hard, when the responsibilities of work and ministry and family start to overwhelm me. Times when I find myself so busy doing God's work that I start to drift away from him. The demands on my time crush and bend and pull me away from my Lord. At every turn I find myself burdened with more work, more busyness, more diversions from God's presence.

I love what I do and how God works through my life and testimony, but sometimes I find myself longing to go back—back to simpler times, back to my days at Teen Challenge, long before anyone knew who I was. Back to my days of ministering on the streets of New York, of preaching on the streets, taking in drug addicts and prostitutes and gang members, helping the most helpless. There was no fame, no glory, no large staff to deal with, no stadiums filled with people. Just me and the kids on the street. The kids who needed someone to talk to. Back then I had no money and no notoriety, but I had all I needed. I had Jesus!

So often I would find a small corner of our building and just sit and talk to God. I would sing to him and whisper my words of love. I would bask in his presence. I would weep with joy as he showered my heart with his favor. Those were simpler and precious times in my life, and I cherish the memories with a passion.

I know what David was going through. I've taken wrong detours. I've sinned against my Lord. I've disappointed him. I don't always stay on the path that he has set before me. But God knows my heart. He knows how much I love and adore him. And when I stray he always brings me back. He always comes to my side, pulling me back beneath the robe of his grace and goodness. He always forgives.

From the moment I gave my heart to Jesus, I've known how little I was capable of bringing to our relationship. There are so many people more talented than me, more eloquent in the pulpit, more smooth in their delivery, more knowledgeable in theology. People with greater gifts to lay at the feet of Jesus. But what I do bring is a heart that is completely and wholly sold out to his kindness! I'm so in love with Jesus that at times I feel as if my chest will burst from my body. My bones aren't large enough to contain my adoration. My vocabulary can't express the depth of my worship! My words can never do justice to the love and devotion I feel in my heart! There are times when I cry in agony because I can't fully express my love!

When I read the psalms of David, I feel such a kinship. I wish I had his ability to communicate his feelings for God with such eloquence and grace. I wish I could write like him. Play the harp as he could play. I can't say that I share his talent, but I do think I share his heart. I know what he was going through. I understand what he must have felt, sitting alone in his cold, dark palace, longing for simpler days. Longing for God's nearness and favor.

And that's why God loved him so. That's why God called David a man after his own heart.

Can you imagine a greater compliment? Can you think of something God could possibly say about someone to bring more weight? God loved David's heart. He connected with him. The two were one in the most intimate and powerful way possible. God related to David, not because of his looks or deeds or strength, but because of the state of his heart. The love in his spirit.

Is there a higher level of communion with our Creator? Can a person get any closer to God than to share the intimacy and thoughts of her heart? Don't we all long to have God say to us, "I love your heart!"?

FORFEITING GOD'S BLESSING

God forgave David for his sin, but look at the blessings David forfeited by falling. Look at what he gave up for his affair with Bathsheba, the hidden cost he paid for detouring from the path that God laid before him. "I anointed you king over Israel," God said to David, "and I delivered you from the hand of Saul. I gave your master's house to you, and your master's wives into your arms. I gave you the house of Israel and Judah. *And if all this had been too little, I would have given you even more*" (2 Samuel 12:7-8, emphasis added).

God was waiting in the wings with blessings that David hadn't even imagined, blessings that he longed to shower upon his servant. Blessings that may have been greater than all the things he had ever done for David in the past. Yet because of his sin, David would live and die never knowing what they were. "And if all this had been too little, I would have given you even more," said God.

Nothing pleases God more than showering his children with wonderful blessings. Heaven is filled with glorious mercies just waiting to be released on servants who remain faithful—servants who embrace the covenant that God has created for them who stay true to the will and purpose that he sets before them. And those blessings aren't reserved just for kings and warriors, but for you and me. For anyone who calls God "Father."

But how and when those blessings come remains entirely up to us. It is our obedience that releases them from God's hand and brings them into our lives. We can live in God's will and experience his mercies each day, or we can walk our own path and forfeit them.

Born for a Great Purpose

God revealed a truth to me about my mother several years ago. It was a revelation that saddened me as much as it opened my eyes. From the day my mother was born, God had a glorious future in store for her. She was destined to be a wonderful mother and nurturer. But more than that, she was destined to do great things for God's kingdom.

My mother was gifted with a powerful sense of insight and discernment. She could look at people and tell what they were experiencing and feeling. She was able to get inside someone's soul the way few people can do.

And she was so beautiful and charming. She had striking green eyes and gorgeous features. She was a tiny woman, thin and graceful and attractive. People were immediately drawn to her.

God gifted my mother with endless talent and ability, and he wanted to use her to do mighty things for his kingdom on earth—to reach countless souls for Christ, to raise a good family, to be an exceptional wife and mother.

But Satan kept her from discovering her godly purpose. He seduced and distracted her at an early age, introducing her to the world of the occult, shielding her from the truth of God's Word. By bringing my mother into a dark and evil world, Satan kept her from embracing the blessings that God had in store for her. He bound her, blinded her, and beat her into submission. She lived most of her life in chains—imprisoned by the Evil One, completely unaware of the goodness and mercy of God.

The day my mother broke free from Satan's curse was the day that she finally began to see what God had planned for her life. She became a different person. Her eyes were opened for the first time, and she could see! She saw the hate and violence that she had lived with, and it was abhorrent to her. It sickened her to think of the way she had treated her family, the love she had withheld, the sin that had held her hostage.

Those beautiful green eyes that had once looked at me with such vengeance and hate were suddenly filled with love. The tension in her face lifted, and a tremendous peace came over her. Jesus came into her heart and took away every ounce of fear, every hint of hate, every lasting shade of darkness and despair. He changed her completely. Finally my mother was able to embrace her purpose, her calling, her glorious future before God.

For the final twenty-five years of my mother's life, she lived in God's blessing and favor. She became the person he had created her to become. She became a wonderful wife and mother. Everyone she met was blessed by her kindness. Friends didn't even recognize her. She was no longer the person whom I had grown up with. Her life was completely transformed by Jesus.

It was only during the final years of her life that my mother was able to see God's covenantal plan for her. The wisdom and insight he imparted into her spirit began to grow and bloom and develop. My mother was able to help and minister to so many people during that time—people who were always amazed at her level of understanding.

I once discovered for myself just how wise my mother could be. Often Gloria and I would go to stay with her and visit, and I noticed how my mother was trying so hard to be kind to Gloria. She would bend over backward to compliment her. The minute Gloria walked into a room, my mother would be by her side, stroking her arm and saying kind things to her. "You look so pretty today, Gloria," she would say. "You're such a good wife to Nicky."

Gloria was often embarrassed by the way she showered her with compliments. I was sure that my mother was simply trying to make up for the years that she had been so angry and vengeful, so one day I took her aside to talk about it. "You know how much Gloria and I love you," I told her, "and our children love you too. You don't have to work to earn our love. We love you just the way you are."

She smiled and said to me, "Son, the reason I'm so nice to your wife is because I know that she will treat you the same way I treat her. If I love her, I know that you will always have her love as well."

It was a bit of wisdom that I will never forget. And it's just one example of the keen insight and discernment that God bestowed upon my mother.

But it still angers me to think of the many years she was robbed of accepting her godly purpose.

MOVING IN GOD'S BLESSING

"Have mercy on me, O God, according to your unfailing love," David prayed on the heels of his sin, "according to your great compassion blot out my transgressions. Wash away all my iniquity and cleanse me from my sin. For I know my transgressions, and my sin is always before me.... Hide your face from my sins and blot out all my iniquity. Create in me a pure heart, O God, and renew a steadfast spirit within me" (Psalm 51:1-3,9-10).

David's sin took him farther from God's face than he ever imagined he could travel. The greatest pain of his life came during his time away from God's hand of blessing and favor. He couldn't bear the thought of losing his relationship with the one he loved the most.

"Do not cast me from your presence or take your Holy Spirit from me. Restore to me the joy of your salvation and grant me a willing spirit, to sustain me" (verses 11-12).

David paid dearly for his sin, but he didn't allow it to define him. When he came to his senses he cried out to God for forgiveness, and God eagerly took him back. But that didn't erase the consequences his sin brought about.

Satan's greatest pleasure on earth comes from keeping souls from accepting God's covenantal blessings. From throwing stumbling blocks in front of God's people to cause them to fall.

If we knew the consequences of our sin before falling to temptation, how many of us would ever take that fatal leap? What a deterrent it would be to see the future—to see the harm that we would be bringing upon ourselves and others. If only we could see beforehand the harm that our sins eventually bring.

No matter how high you stand in God's favor, how blessed your life has been, how close to God you've felt in your life, sin can bring you down and crush you. It can devastate your life and your relationship with God. It can pull you farther from God than you ever dreamed of traveling. Sin will destroy you. Persecute you. Alienate you. Hound you. Defeat you. If you let it.

And it can happen quicker than you ever dreamed possible.

That's why living in the blessing of God demands that we discover the covenant he has prepared for us. That we seek the purpose he has set before us. And that we always look to the future. Calculate the cost of every decision. Keep our eyes fixed firmly on the path that God has set before us and stay focused and true. Understand the dangers of detouring from the covenant that God has given us.

CHAPTER SIXTEEN

ENGAGING GOD'S COVENANTS

I've often wondered why our ministry isn't in bankruptcy. For all practical purposes we should have had to close our doors years ago. We've never been good at fund-raising, and I hate asking people for money. When I speak, I never plead for support. A lot of times pastors will want to take an offering for our ministry, and I allow them to do so, but only if they agree to keep it short and simple, and never after I speak. I don't want anything interfering with the altar call. Collections can be distracting to sinners, and I try to be extremely sensitive to that fact. Many people are convinced that all evangelists are greedy, and I never want anyone to say that about our work.

Throughout my years as an evangelist to the inner city, I've never done things the proper way. Our ministry doesn't have a bunch of rich supporters that we cater to, and we never wine and dine celebrities in order to raise money.

Just recently we turned over our mailing department to an outside firm, and they were shocked to see how disorganized our fund-raising campaign had been. We had very few names in our database and almost never kept track of supporters in an effort to gain their continued support. "How have you survived all these years?" they asked us with a stunned look. I didn't know what to tell them.

The truth is, we simply trust God day to day, and he has always taken care of us. When we're short of funds, we don't panic and get on the phone, we get on our knees and pray. When we need money for a crusade that God has led us to organize, we book a coliseum and trust God to bring in the funds to pay for it. If people tried to run a business the way we run our ministry, the bankers would laugh them out of the office.

But I wouldn't have it any other way. This is God's ministry, and what I do is his work, and he is the only supporter we need. If he wants us to survive and continue, he will bring in the money for us to do so. If not, he will let us know, and we'll close our doors.

God's blessing on our ministry is what shows me that we are staying on course and in his will. His hand of provision is the litmus test we use to know that we are remaining true to our covenant. I could spend half my time putting together projection sheets and fund-raising flyers and working to attract contributors, but none of that would matter if I wasn't doing exactly what God wanted me to do. This is his ministry, not mine. He sets my agenda. He pays my bills. He provides what we need. He tells us where to go and how to minister. He puts the messages on my heart and leads me to the people who need to hear those messages.

God is the one who made this covenant with me, and he is the one who keeps it fresh and alive. I'm not here to please men, only Jesus.

WHEN GOD PROVIDES

There is a tremendous amount of relief in living under the guidance and provision of God. It takes a lot of worry off your shoulders. I don't have to wonder where my next meal is coming from or whether I'll have a place to lay my head. I know that God is in complete control. And God has never let me down.

Early in my ministry I worried about my children. I knew that my background would haunt me, and I wondered if the curse my parents were under would bleed over into my family. I knew that Satan didn't like the way I assaulted him week after week and the way I did it in his own backyard. He taunted me constantly, and I knew he would do the same to my wife and children.

As an evangelist I spent a lot of time on the road, away from home, and as a young man I spent hours praying that God would take care of my family, protect them from the harm that Satan wanted to do to them. I was no stranger to the devil's wrath. My fear was well founded.

So many nights I lay awake in a hotel room praying, "Lord, you know that I try to be the best husband and father I can be. I love my children and Gloria more than I love my own life. I couldn't stand the thought of anything happening to them. Please take care of my family. Please watch over them while I'm gone. Don't let Satan come to them in my absence and steal their hearts. Watch over my babies, Jesus."

The more I prayed that prayer, the more God would put a sense of peace in my spirit. He told me that if I would stay faithful to his calling on my life, he would take care of Gloria and the children. He knew my heart. He knew how much I wanted to serve him and how much I hurt for the lost and helpless of the world, so he commissioned me to reach out to them at every opportunity. And he wanted me to do so without worrying about my family.

It was one of the many covenants that God has made with me through the years. He promised to take care of my family, so I released them completely to his care. And he has always kept his promise.

TAKE CARE OF MY BABY!

I remember when Gloria was pregnant with our second daughter, Nicole. The pregnancy had been a difficult one, and Nicole didn't arrive on time. I had worked my schedule so that I could be there for her birth, but she was a week late. I had committed to speaking at an event in Lansing, Michigan, so I booked a quick flight and told Gloria I would be back the day after the crusade.

I hated leaving Gloria in such a condition, but I knew God would take care of her. And I hoped that I'd be back before our daughter was born.

The night of the crusade I looked out over the stadium and it was filled to the brim. Every seat was taken, and I was praying before my talk, asking God to bless my testimony. Then just minutes before I was to go on stage a phone call came for me. A nurse told me that Gloria had gone into labor and had been taken to the hospital. She didn't want to bother me until after the crusade, but something had gone wrong during the delivery. Nicole was a breach delivery and didn't come out as quickly as she should have.

An ambulance had rushed Nicole to a nearby children's hospital, and she was in bad condition. "She may not live," the nurse told me. My hands were shaking as I hung up the phone. In the background I could hear a man onstage introducing me as the speaker. My mind was racing with fear and worry. *What do I do? How can I go on the stage with this hanging over my head? I need to get home to my family!*

I started to pray. "Lord, what do I do? What's happening to my baby? Please don't let her die! Don't let anything happen to my baby daughter! Please, God." I prayed fervently for wisdom and guidance. I looked up and the man on stage was waiting for me to join him. I didn't know whether to run or burst out crying!

Suddenly a calm came over my spirit. I took a deep breath and let it out. And God spoke to my spirit. *Nicky, I promised I would take care of your family. You know I won't let anything happen to her. She's in my care. Don't worry, Nicky. I'll take care of your baby.*

I took another deep breath to regain my composure and then turned to face the man on stage. *I trust you, Lord,* I prayed. *I'll finish your work here and trust you to take care of my family.*

That evening we experienced a powerful outpouring of God's Spirit. Many lives came to Jesus. And though I still worried about my daughter, I knew she was safe in God's hands. He would take care of her.

Early the next morning I was on a plane back home, and I arrived at the hospital to find that Nicole was still in intensive care. The doctors were not encouraging about her chances, but I knew that she would be all right. I knew that God would take care of her.

Every day in the hospital, our baby Nicole was getting stronger. The hospital bills were also mounting, and Gloria and I knew we had no money to take care of it. But even that we laid at God's feet.

Two weeks later they finally allowed her to come home with us. When the final bill from the hospital arrived, I nearly passed out from the shock.

I knew it would be expensive, but I suddenly got a crash course in the high cost of medicine!

Still, God took care of it, just as he always had.

No Fear of Flying

Most people would be surprised to learn that I once had a terrible fear of flying. Since I spend so many hours on a plane each week, this may sound hard to believe.

As a young man I had no problem with planes. And then one day I was traveling with David Wilkerson to see our good friend Kathryn Kuhlman speak at a crusade. We were traveling from New York to Pittsburgh, and along the way I noticed that David was white as a sheet. He was holding on to the armrest tightly, sweat pouring down the sides of his face.

"What's wrong?" I asked him, thinking he might be having a heart attack.

"I'm okay," he said. "I just don't like flying too much. I've heard a lot of stories about planes going down, and I don't want to die this way. I'll be all right, just give me a few minutes to calm down."

Before that time I never worried much about flying, but I remember thinking, *If David is so afraid of flying, maybe it's more dangerous than I thought. David isn't afraid of anything! He faced our gang down without batting an eye, but now he's white as a sheet.*

Over the next few months I began to develop a terrible fear of flying. And I often prayed to God, "Please don't let me die on an airplane. I'm not through raising my family. I'm not through serving you. I don't want to die young... I want to grow old with Gloria and the kids."

The more I prayed this prayer, the more fearful I became. It was beginning to become a real phobia with me. I knew I couldn't continue traveling so much if I didn't deal with this fear, but I couldn't seem to get past it.

Then one day I was praying fervently, "Lord, please do something to take away this fear. I don't know what to do, but every time I get on a plane I get frightened. Show me what you want me to do and I'll do it."

For a long time I felt no answer, and then suddenly the Lord put a strong sense of release in my spirit. He told me, *Nicky, I have a lot of plans for you, and I'm not going to let you die in an airplane. You don't have to worry. Just trust me, and I'll take care of you.*

The sense of his voice was so strong that from that moment on I no longer feared airplanes. I knew in my heart that God had made this covenant with me, and it completely freed me to relax during flights. Since that day I've had numerous close calls on planes. I've been through horrible weather and lightning and wind shears on all types of airplanes, but never have I been fearful. I simply say to God, *You made a promise, and I trust you. Even if we lose our engines and go down, I know I'll survive, because you promised me I wouldn't die on an airplane.*

I remember once when this new sense of bravery was tested. I had been speaking at a crusade in South Africa and was flying back home to North Carolina. About halfway through the flight, we heard strange popping noises coming from the hull. We had no idea what was going on, and the passengers began to get nervous. The pilot finally came over the intercom to tell us that we were being shot at by rebels from Angola. The bullets were hitting the underside of the plane.

The man seated next to me panicked. He was about three hundred pounds, and he tried to climb over me to get out of his seat. I'm not a large man, and I was pinned beneath him. I couldn't breathe or talk, and he continued to push his way out into the aisle. I had to do something, so I doubled up my fist and punched him in the windpipe with the butt of my elbow. He gasped for air and then sat back in his seat. "Relax," I told him. "Nothing is going to happen to us. I'm a minister, and God told me years ago that I would never die in an airplane, so stop worrying. As long as I'm on the plane, nothing can happen to you."

He looked at me as if I were crazy. But at least he stopped panicking. The strangest thing was, I was telling him the truth. I honestly had no fear of dying, even though everyone on the plane was in a dire panic.

The pilot came on again and told us he was turning the plane around and heading back to Johannesburg. Before long we were surrounded by military planes escorting our plane back to safety.

Some people may think it's foolish to feel so calm in the midst of danger, but God's promises are as real to me as the skin around my bones. When he tells me something, I believe him. When he says he will protect me, I put fear out of my mind. When God makes a covenant with someone, he never breaks his promises.

Protected on Satan's Turf

The ministry that God has called me to is not your average missionary work. What we do would be considered dangerous and unhealthy by many evangelists. Downright nuts might be a better description!

We go after lost souls in some of the most dangerous areas of the world. And we often plant ourselves in the heart of the most dangerous neighborhoods of those areas. We save souls by reaching into Satan's mouth and snatching them out of his crooked jaws. Like David Wilkerson, we stand on the edge of hell and throw our line into the fire to save lost children from doom.

It's not safe work. The neighborhoods we walk are often places where policemen are afraid to go—places where gangs rule the roost and places that decent people avoid. And the reason we do this is because God has called us for this purpose. This is my mission field, because this is where God came to save me.

Throughout the years I have never shied away from taking my children—and now my grandchildren—into the streets with us. When we would set up a Hit 'n' Run outreach in a gang-infested neighborhood, my kids would be right there beside me, helping set up speakers and passing out tracts or Bibles on the street. Today they bring their husbands and young children with them. Our family has learned to have no fear of harm. No fear of Satan and his wily little demons. No fear of the neighborhood thugs who come around and scowl. We take precautions, but we never cower.

People might think this strange, but I know that God watches over us. God will never allow us to be harmed.

Years ago, before we ever started our outreach to inner cities, the Lord told me that he would never allow harm to come to me or my family during our crusades. He told me that if I would be faithful to my calling, he would be faithful to this promise. His covenant was clear, and so we set out on our mission in complete trust.

People are surprised when I tell them that no harm has ever come to anyone during one of our inner-city outreaches. We've held literally thousands of Hit 'n' Run events around the world, in the most frightening places imaginable, often with just a small group of kids, but nothing has ever happened. Every day kids are shot down in these neighborhoods, simply for looking at someone the wrong way, yet we come uninvited, with speakers blaring a message that directly confronts their lifestyle, and walk away unfazed. Never once have they harmed us. Never once has anyone gone away with a scratch. Never once has Satan been able to touch me, my family, or anyone working to help us.

It's not as if he hasn't tried. We've experienced threats and intimidation a number of times. Gangs have surrounded us, taunted us, laughed at us, threatened us, but they've never been able to touch us. God has not allowed them to. My kids have always been safe, and I've always been confident that they would be.

BELIEVING GOD

God's covenantal promises are as real and secure as any truth we can imagine. When God makes a promise to us, it is not only certain but irrevocable. And he loves making covenants with his children.

But God's covenants demand action on our part. He doesn't make covenants with idle, double-minded people. He wants people who will trust him, obey him, engage with him on a daily basis. God wants to speak with us, and he wants us to speak back. To listen, to ask questions, and to answer when he speaks. God isn't passive, and he doesn't want passive followers!

If we listen we can hear God talking, trying to engage us. Trying to get a message through and a response back. But so often we miss it. Either we're not hearing, or we don't believe that God is really interested in talking with us.

In the book of 1 Kings, God's prophet Micaiah told King Ahab of a vision he had had from the Lord. Micaiah described his dream to Ahab, saying, "I saw the LORD sitting on his throne with all the host of heaven standing around him on his right and on his left. And the LORD said, 'Who will entice Ahab into attacking Ramoth Gilead and going to his death there?'

"One suggested this, and another that. Finally, a spirit came forward, stood before the LORD and said, 'I will entice him.'

" 'By what means?' the LORD asked.

" 'I will go out and be a lying spirit in the mouths of all his prophets,' he said.

" 'You will succeed in enticing him,' said the LORD. 'Go and do it' " (22:19-22).

Micaiah witnessed God engaging with his heavenly spirits the same way he wants to engage with his people. God wants to talk to us, to ask us questions, to get us thinking and talking back with him. He gave us a free will for a reason. He doesn't want puppets that just wait for him to pull our strings before we move—he wants thinking, feeling, caring, passionate people to respond to him, interact with him, engage him in conversation.

"How long will these people treat me with contempt?" the Lord asked Moses (Numbers 14:11). And I don't think his question was a rhetorical one! He wanted an answer from Israel. He wanted them to engage him in conversation. He wanted action!

ENGAGING GOD

When God speaks, he wants us to respond. To answer. To do something. To acknowledge his voice and speak back.

And he only speaks to people who are willing to listen.

Too often we spend our days in lifeless, passionless pursuits. We live day to day, aimlessly waiting on God to give us some direction, some guidance, some word of prophecy. We want to follow God, but we have no idea where he is leading us.

I see this every day—in people, in churches, in businesses, in ministries, in every area of life. So many long to hear God and to engage with him in a covenantal relationship, but nothing ever happens. God's voice never comes. His leading never becomes clear.

But we serve a God of passion—a God of action. A God who longs for servants obsessed with obedience, preoccupied with discovering his will, completely enamored with the thought of living and dying in God's holy presence!

That's what God is looking for. And when he finds it, he always takes notice!

CHAPTER SEVENTEEN

IN THE BLESSING OF GOD

I'm always amazed at how much fun it is to move in the blessing of God. When God directs your path, it's always exhilarating and seldom what you might expect. It's never boring, never predictable, never ordinary, and always invigorating.

I've spent more than forty years traveling and ministering, following God wherever he leads. In that time I've taken a lot of detours. At times I've failed him, but I always come back. At other times I've seen God work in ways that are too awesome for words. God has displayed the power of his Spirit and his Word so many times that I've long since given up trying to second-guess him. When the Holy Spirit guides your path, the best you can do is hang on and try your best to keep up.

There's nothing about this life that I would change. I often get tired of traveling, but I never get tired of seeing God work. Every time I get on an airplane I know it's going to be another adventure with God. "Where are you going to take me today?" I ask Jesus. "I can't wait to see what surprises you have in store!"

And he never disappoints me.

ANOTHER ADVENTURE BEGINS

Several years ago I was invited to speak at a crusade in Hawaii during Thanksgiving and another in Guam shortly afterward. I thought I would use the opportunity to take my family to Hawaii on vacation during the holidays. We almost always spend Thanksgiving at home, but this would be a good chance to spend a few days on the island together. I had spoken in Hawaii several times, but we'd never been there on vacation.

My family was so excited about the trip. I still remember Gloria beaming as we walked through the airport to the Continental terminal. We checked our bags and boarded the plane, then off we went.

We landed in Honolulu at around ten in the evening and went straight to the baggage claim area. The passengers were all smiling and laughing, just excited to finally be on the ground. Flying to Hawaii is different from most destinations. Something about the island just excites people, and there's always a sense of exuberance in the air—probably because most passengers are there to play, not work.

When we reached the baggage area, I was surprised by how little security there was. This was the early nineties, and security wasn't as tight as it is today, but it still was a bit odd that no one was watching the bags or doors.

It seemed to take forever for the bags to come. Things were obviously running behind schedule. People were starting to get antsy. But suddenly the belt started moving, and luggage started to appear through the chute.

One by one the bags came, and we watched anxiously for our suitcases to arrive.

To one side I noticed two African American men who looked strangely suspicious. Something about their demeanor didn't seem quite right. They were waiting for bags, just like all the other passengers, but I didn't remember seeing them on the plane. And they seemed to be watching the people more than the baggage belt.

People were bustling back and forth all around me, all in a hurry to get their bags and get to their hotels. The earlier light mood seemed to have left us, and now everyone seemed more aggravated by the delay.

One of our bags came through the chute, and I quickly grabbed it from the belt and set it beside Gloria, then again watched for the rest of our luggage. Suddenly there was a commotion to one side. The two suspicious men I had noticed earlier were trying to help an American woman with her bags, and she didn't seem too excited about the help. She had her suitcase by one end, and one of the men had it by the other. They were pulling against each other. While this was going on, I noticed the other man behind her with his hand in her purse.

The two were professional pickpockets. One was creating a diversion while the other slipped her wallet from her purse. I saw the whole thing, and a large African American woman just across from me saw it as well, because she started screaming and pointing at the men. "He got her wallet!" she screamed over and over. "That man took her wallet out of her purse!"

The two men panicked and started to run. Everyone stopped what they were doing and craned their necks to see what was happening. The woman kept screaming and pointing as the men ran toward the exit.

I grew up on the streets, and I knew instinctively that the best thing to do in a robbery is let them take what they want and leave. Your life is more important than a little money. Nothing good can come of trying to stop a thief in panic. They'll use whatever means necessary to get away—whether it's a gun, a knife, or just a rock. Crooks are most dangerous when they're fleeing for their lives. I know this from firsthand experience. I've been there more times than I care to remember. The best thing to do is to get a good look at their faces and clothes so that you can describe them to the police later.

I knew this because I grew up on the streets. But Gloria didn't. Gloria just saw a crime being committed, and she wanted someone to stop them. She wanted *me* to stop them!

"Nicky," Gloria screamed at the top of her lungs, "go after them. Nicky why are you standing there? Go get them!"

I tried to signal her to calm down, but she just kept screaming and pointing. "Nicky, aren't you going to do something?"

Suddenly everyone was looking at me! The other woman was still screaming and pointing and so was Gloria. Nobody dared move, but they all looked at me, as if to say, "Yeah, Nicky. Aren't you going to do something about this?"

I'm still not sure why I did it, but I went after them. Mostly from embarrassment. I didn't want to look like a chicken. But even as I ran after the men, I remember thinking, *What are you doing? You're going to get yourself killed!*

Adrenaline must have been rushing through my veins, because I caught up with one of the men within a few minutes. Just as I reached out for him, the other man threw the woman's wallet down and took off in another direction. I grabbed the man by the back of his coat and threw him up against a brick wall, then held him up against it. I still wasn't sure why I had gone after them, but now that I had caught one, I knew I needed to be forceful. He was a large man, nearly twice my size, and the last thing I wanted to do was get into some kind of wrestling match with him. So I did the first thing that came to mind. I pretended to be a detective.

"Spread your legs," I shouted, as forcefully as I could. "Arms against the wall. And don't move or I'll splatter your brains all over the place!"

The man didn't know what to do. I could feel him shaking, and he kept saying, "Don't hurt me, sir. I won't move. Just don't hurt me!"

I shoved my hand into his back and pushed him even harder against the wall. Instinct told me I couldn't show any fear and that I needed to remain intimidating. Though everything in my bones was telling me I was crazy for taking such a chance.

"I've been watching you," I said with a snarl. "I've got no patience for your kind. Keep your hands up and your legs spread until my backup gets here. Don't make me do anything rash!"

The whole time the young man was pleading for me not to hurt him. "Please let me go," he said. "I won't do it again, I promise. My friend made me do it. I'll never rob anyone again. Just give me a break. Please let me go!"

I had no idea whether anyone had called the police or not, but I wasn't about to take any chances. I told him, "Look, kid. I'm going to give you a break and let you go. But don't ever let me see you around here again! You got it? You run away and just keep running if you know what's good for you!"

"Thank you, sir. I'll never do it again. Thank you," he said, still trembling. I turned him loose, and he ran away faster than I thought his legs could carry him. He was scared to death. And I was relieved that no one had been hurt. Especially me!

STILL ALIVE!

I was quiet in the car all the way to the hotel. Quite honestly, I was still a bit shaken as well as irritated with Gloria for getting me involved in the incident. We also had Elena with us, and I didn't want her to know what had happened.

But while we were checking into the hotel, Gloria said to me, "Nicky, I had no idea you were so brave. I've never seen you like that. I was so proud of you!"

"Brave," I said. "That was the stupidest thing I've ever done. You should be thanking God that you're not a widow right now. Do you know how dangerous that was? He was younger than me and stronger than me, and he probably had a knife or a gun. I could have been killed!"

Gloria looked stunned. And I was a little ashamed that I got upset with her. But I knew how dangerous my actions had been, and I was still irritated at her for screaming for me to get involved.

I'm not sure Gloria believed me at the time, but when she told the story later to Sonny Arguinzoni, he had the same reaction I had. "Gloria, you're lucky you're not a widow right now," he told her. "I would think that Nicky knows better than to go after a crook on the run. He could have been killed!"

Sonny grew up on the streets, just as I had, so he understood the dangers. I could tell that hearing it from Sonny made a big impact on Gloria. I'm not sure she'll be so quick to get me involved in another mugging.

Looking back on the incident, I'm amazed that I didn't show better sense. I could have just looked the other way and explained to Gloria later why I didn't go after them. My family is more important than a woman's wallet. But pride got in the way, causing me to do the stupidest thing I could have done. God protected me anyway; in spite of my foolishness, he sent an angel to watch over me.

I can almost imagine him saying, "Okay, Nicky, now that you've got all this machismo out of your system, let's get back to work. But don't ever try that again!"

A Fateful Typhoon

Thanksgiving came and I preached at the coliseum to a wonderful response. It was a great outpouring of God's Spirit.

My family had a great time vacationing in Hawaii, but then it came time to go to Guam.

A few nights before our flight, we saw on the news that a typhoon was on its way to Guam, and it was scheduled to hit just two days before our crusade. I wondered if the crusade might be canceled but hadn't heard anything before our flight, so I decided to fly in and see what they had planned.

The typhoon was one of the worst in Guam's history. It hit the island dead center. Our plane circled the airport numerous times, looking for an opportunity to land. We were afraid that the plane would be detoured, but the pilot persisted until he found a small break in the winds, taking us quickly down to the runway.

The plane stopped several hundred feet from the terminal, and the flight attendant told us that we'd have to get our luggage together and walk. "Be careful," she told us, "because the steps are slippery."

I gathered up my coat and briefcase and walked behind a woman with two kids in tow. I remember watching the kids to make sure they didn't fall. Several people ahead of me were slipping, and I remember watching them, wondering if they were going to fall. Suddenly my foot slipped out from under me. I fell flat on my behind, and my briefcase flew into the air. It hit the ground and opened, causing papers and books and folders to fly everywhere. Every passenger on board stopped to look in my direction.

There I sat on the wet floor with my stuff scattered everywhere. "I'm all right," I kept saying. "Don't worry, nothing's broken." Inside I was reeling from embarrassment.

I picked myself up and wiped off my pants as best I could, but a huge stain ran down the rear of my slacks. I don't embarrass easily, but this is one time I truly felt like crawling under a rock.

I got to the hotel to find that no one in the area had running water. The typhoon had done tremendous damage to the utility plant, and they didn't expect it to come on for several days—maybe longer.

It was still unclear whether we would be able to have our crusade. The stadium had been hit hard by the typhoon, and there was no way they'd be able to have it ready in time, but the governor continued to tell me that he was going to work something out. "I want people to hear you speak," he told me, though he had no idea how that would be possible. I told him I was available for whatever he needed me to do.

For two days I stayed in the hotel room with no water. I couldn't shave or bathe, and I was getting cabin fever from waiting. I remember feeling very discouraged and praying, "Lord, why did you bring me here? I embarrassed myself at the airport, I look terrible, and the stadium is closed. What good am I doing here?"

SMALL MIRACLES

The next day I woke up and still didn't have water in the room. I'd gotten word that the governor was working out a place for the crusade, so I assumed

I'd be speaking somewhere. I hadn't exercised in a few days and was feeling antsy, so I decided to run down to the beach and wash up in the ocean. I figured I would take a small towel with me and go on a run through the streets of Guam for ten or twelve miles and then make my way over to the ocean.

During my run I got a good glimpse of what the typhoon had done to the island. The streets and yards were filled with mud and dirt, and many were impassable. I couldn't imagine that anyone would be interested in coming to my crusade after what had happened. I didn't even know how they would get there. Most public transportation wasn't running, and people were busy cleaning up their properties. The more I ran, the more discouraged I became.

I ended my run at the beach, but before going into the water I sat in the sand to rest and reflect on what I had seen. I was still unsure why God had brought me to Guam in the middle of a disaster. And I wasn't looking forward to spending the rest of the day itching after washing up in salt water.

"Lord, why can't I have a place to wash up?" I prayed. "I know it's a silly thing to ask for, but I need a shave and a bath, and I don't want to give my testimony stinking of ocean water, with my hair salty and matted."

Even as I prayed I remember thinking that it was a trivial thing to ask for. Surely God is more interested in what I say than whether I've had a bath or not. I mean, look at John the Baptist. He probably smelled bad all the time, and look how much good he did!

I began feeling bad about complaining, knowing that many on the island were in much worse shape than I was. Many had lost homes and cars, and all I'd lost was the privilege of bathing for a few days. "Lord," I prayed. "forgive me for being selfish. I'm here to reach people with your message, and I'll do whatever it takes to do that. Use me however you need. I won't complain anymore."

Just then I laid back in the sand, propping myself up with my elbows. I poked the ground harder than expected and felt something cold and wet on my left elbow. I leaned over to look and saw a small puddle of water where my elbow had been. *That's strange,* I thought. *I'm too far from the ocean to strike water.*

I dug into the sand a little deeper, and the more I dug, the more the water sprang up out of the ground. I cupped some in my hand and smelled it. *That's not salt water.* I dug deeper with my palms, and soon a huge puddle of water was bubbling out of the ground—fresh spring water! It was like a well, just inches below the surface. There was no explanation for it—no rivers or ponds nearby. And it was clean and clear.

I crouched down on my knees and started washing my face and hands in it. I scooped a little up in my fingers and tasted it with my tongue. It was wonderful—like bottled water. So I began washing my hair and shaving and cleaning under my arms.

"Is this from you, Lord?" I prayed, almost not believing that God would provide such a blessing for me. "Thank you, Jesus! Thank you for this clean water."

As I was bathing and playing in the fresh spring well, some people on the beach came to see what was going on. They couldn't believe their eyes. "Where did this water come from?" they asked, but I didn't know what to tell them. Several offered to pay me if I'd let them bathe in it, but I laughed and told them, "It's not my water. It's from the Lord. There's plenty for everyone!"

All over the beach people were coming to bathe in the new spring that God had provided. Before long there was a line formed down the beach,

each person waiting his turn. I still don't know where the spring came from, only that God saw fit to provide this small, unexpected blessing for me and the others along the beach.

That's the fun of living with God. You never know what he's going to do next. You just know that whatever he does will be exciting!

GOD WILL PROVIDE

There wasn't a coliseum in all of Guam that was open, and the governor was running out of options for our venue. For a time it looked as if we were just going to have to cancel the crusade. But at the last minute he convinced the owners of the largest shopping mall on the island to close early and let me speak on the main floor.

That evening people packed into the mall from all over the island. I wasn't sure the mall would be able to hold everyone. They filled up every corner of the main hallway and overflowed into the side halls as well. Thousands of people packed into the relatively small area.

The governor had a stage and equipment brought in and set up in the middle of the mall, and that's where I gave my testimony. Afterward, during the altar call, people came forward from every corner of the mall. Many had simply come that day to do some shopping and found themselves in the middle of a church service, convicted by the Holy Spirit to turn their lives around. Hundreds of people were saved that day. The governor and his wife were near tears. "This is a refreshing time for our island," he told me. "Thank you for coming."

I was so exhilarated by what the Lord had done. I laughed aloud and told the governor, "This trip has been one of the greatest adventures of my life. I nearly got killed playing private investigator in Hawaii, I made a fool of myself in the Guam airport, and I got to shower in a miracle spring at the beach. I'm not sure what God is trying to teach me, but it's certainly been interesting. I just wonder what he has planned next."

I've always said that people who follow the Spirit's leading are never bored, and time and time again God proves me right. Moving in the blessing of God is anything but bland. You never know where he will take you, what he will teach you, how he will use you, or what miracles he will bring your way.

If you don't have that in your life, don't go another day without finding it. Don't live one more minute without experiencing the life-changing power of the Holy Spirit. Don't spend another second outside of God's anointed blessing. When God directs your path, life is never, ever the same.

THE ULTIMATE BLESSING

You and I have been given a gift greater than we could ever imagine or ask for. We've been entrusted with the most powerful blessing we could ever receive. It is the gift of the Holy Spirit. God's Spirit. The Spirit that *is* God, that lives within us, directing us, guiding us, empowering us for great and mighty things.

And with this gift comes great responsibility. We are to take this gift and use it for God's glory. Use it to *further* God's glory, to further the work of the kingdom.

When we move in the blessing of God, we can never forget the source of this blessing nor the reason he blesses us. It's not to keep us comfortable, but to empower us for even greater service.

No one is more obsessed with saving souls than God. His heart burns for those who need his love and forgiveness, for those who refuse to trust him with their future, for those who have yet to understand just how much he loves and cares for them, how much he wants to hold them in his loving arms, kiss away the pain, and bring them into the fold of eternity!

God lives to see the day that heaven is literally bursting at the seams with souls, and he has trusted you and me to see that that happens. He has put his faith in us to carry this burden for him, to carry his message of hope to a lost world. He longs for us to develop a soul obsession in the depths of our heart.

If you haven't embraced the passion for souls that God wants each of us to have—the passion that Jesus displayed during his days on earth—then begin today by asking God to burn it into your heart.

If you haven't developed a heart of mercy for those who need Jesus, then pray for a burden in your soul. Pray that God would help you see people the way that Jesus sees them.

If you haven't received a vision from God, a covenant from God, a sense of his purpose for your life, then go to your knees and stay there until you get one. Petition God, plead with him, beg him, hound him until you get a clear sense of your specific purpose within his great plan and his will for you to achieve this vision.

Give your whole heart to God, and he will ignite within you a soul obsession greater than you ever dreamed you could have. He will give you a burden for those who need Jesus. And then he will give you all the tools you need to reach them. He will work through you more mightily, more powerfully, more supernaturally than even your boldest prayers could conceive.

Trust God, believe God, love God, depend on God, give everything you are and have to God, and you will move in the blessing of God.

ACKNOWLEDGMENTS

I have several people I'd like to thank for helping with this book.

First, thanks to Alicia and Patrick, my daughter and son-in-law, for helping us compile information and for blessing me with their lives.

To Karen Robinson, for the hours she spent reading the manuscript and catching our mistakes, often on her own time, to help make this a better book.

To Dr. James Derickson, my personal physician and friend. He is a doctor who truly cares for his patients, not just for their bodies, but for their hearts. He has spiritual insight as well as professional knowledge, and that makes him an exceptional healer and friend. He has taken a real interest in my life and ministry, as well as my health, and for that I am eternally grateful.

Finally to Gloria, my sweet wife, for reminding me of many of the stories and facts we needed to include in this manuscript. At times I didn't want to write about an event, but she convinced me that I should.

ABOUT THE AUTHORS

Nicky Cruz is the best-selling author of seventeen books, including the all-time Christian classic, *Run Baby Run*, now in its thirty-seventh year of publication in forty-three languages worldwide. It is still a top-ten best-seller in the United Kingdom. His most recent book is *One Holy Fire: Let the Spirit Ignite Your Soul.*

Nicky is a minister and evangelist who has reached tens of millions of people around the globe with his powerful testimony. He is the president of Nicky Cruz Outreach, and he is the founder of TRUCE, an international discipleship ministry dedicated to reaching and mentoring young people around the globe. Each year he speaks to more than five hundred thousand people in stadiums and venues throughout the world. *The Wall Street Journal* described Nicky as the "Billy Graham of the streets," a title that aptly describes his influence for Christ

Nicky is the father of four daughters and seven grandchildren. He lives in Colorado Springs with his wife, Gloria. If you would like to learn more about Nicky Cruz Outreach or find out how you can support TRUCE urban evangelism training center, please visit us at www.nickycruz.org.

Frank Martin is an author and commentary writer for Focus on the Family. He collaborated with Nicky Cruz on *One Holy Fire*. Frank and his wife, Ruthie, live in Colorado Springs with their two children. You can visit his Web site at www.frankmartin.com.

What would happen
if you called on God's Spirit
to **unleash his power** in your life?

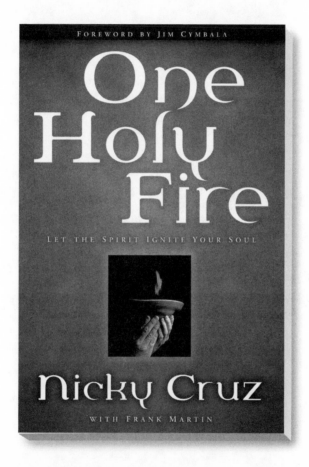

"Nicky Cruz is absolutely on target as he writes of the critical moment of time we live in and the fantastic potential there is in Spirit-filled, Spirit-led believers to extend God's kingdom around the world. One Holy Fire *can change your life and set you ablaze for God."*

—PASTOR JIM CYMBALA, THE BROOKLYN TABERNACLE